The Floor is **not** an Option!

Simple Solutions to Eliminate Clutter

**With Special Instructions for Those with
Attention Deficit Disorders, Dyslexia and Hoarding Issues**

Sheila G. McCurdy

Illustrations by JoAnn Terzano

Sheila G. McCurdy | Publisher

To all of my Clients and those who have named themselves:
"The Plodder — Take two steps forward and one back"
"The Bag Lady — Love My Bags"

Published by
Sheila G. McCurdy
CLUTTER STOP®
PO Box 2014
Upland CA 91785-2014

Copyright © 2002 by Sheila G. McCurdy
Illustrations by JoAnn Terzano
Design by Deborah Laux

ISBN: 0-9716342-0-3

Printed in the USA

TESTIMONIALS

I'm glad I have enough self-esteem to hire Sheila, an expert on organizing – the area I'm weak in. Why would anyone be ashamed to admit that organization is not their strong suit? This is building your staircase to your heavenly reward because there's no price that you can put on this help.
AZ, Upland CA

I've got time - I just have to find it!
LW, Pasadena CA

I had given up any thoughts of ever getting organized...I was going down for the third time. I shut down emotionally and socially. [Now,] I am beginning to have more free space than I ever dreamed possible in such a small apartment. Wow, God is so good! Not only has my apartment been affected, but also my desk at work. I believe that I have one of the most organized desks in the entire building.
RS, Pomona CA

I took one summer off to try and get organized but I couldn't get it under control – not without any help. Things just got away from me, and even if I tried it didn't seem like I was making any progress. Sheila really has helped. She told me I wasn't a pack rat but I needed organizational help. We did all the organizing together, which is great. She has no emotional ties to anything in your house but yet she understands. She asked my permission before we threw anything out. I can come home now and relax. I can invite people to my home without being embarrassed. I've learned how to organize and clean, which aren't the same things. Personally, I feel better than I have in a long time.
JS, Claremont CA

Sheila came over and helped me. I couldn't do it on my own because I was so overwhelmed. I didn't know how to begin. It had been a number of years trying to get it done and now I can get some work done. I love the room and can even open the window without falling into something. I tell everybody and show everybody what I've accomplished. It's so much easier to find things, where before it would take days and then I would give up and find it several days later. Now I know exactly where to look for it.
IA, Mira Loma CA

Special Thanks

To my clients, who have shared the anxiety of waiting for this book and who have been a constant source of inspiration, insight, information, laughter and friendship.

To my readers, Sue Zepeda and Wendy Carey, who have shared the difficult chore of reading different portions of text and giving me feedback. This job was not easy.

To my editor, Abbey Rainey, who has spent untold hours pouring over this text in order to bring it all together. She is a great marvel and a great friend.

To my illustrator, Jo Ann Terzano, who took what I saw in my head and put it on paper, plus using her own feelings and putting them on paper after reading the text.

To my graphic designer, Deborah Laux, who took this epistle to its final step with an absolute "can do" attitude.

Without all of the above, this book wouldn't be. Very personal special thanks go to my husband, Lyle, who quickly came to my aid whenever my computer went nuts and I was having an anxiety attack! As always, he took care of the computer, which decreased my anxiety. He is a special man who has always convinced me to do "my thing."

And to my cheering crowd...my children, Lorrenda and Sue and their spouses, close friends and other organizers who said "Go for it!" and kept me accountable, especially Janice Kemmer.

A million thanks to everyone who had faith that I could do this project and to God for giving me the talent and wisdom to pursue it.

Table of Contents

On the Path to Bright Windows

A Look at Getting Organized

It's said that the eyes are the windows to the soul.

Are your windows bright? Or, are they dull? Is your soul hungering for relief from the clutter, the forgotten appointments, and the lost stuff?

As in the premise of my book, "The Permanent Solution," if you're:

- Ready,
- Willing, and
- Able

You CAN become organized. And you can stay that way – if you're willing.

So, are you ready? Great! We're going to take a journey. We'll start in the rubble-strewn village of Disorganization, where you currently live, and end our journey at the city heights of Organization, where you'll be moving to!

We'll start on the path of our journey by walking through your home, room by room. Don't bother to shove things into cupboards and behind doors. We both know what's there. Don't worry, I won't tell! But, I do promise you something: small "miracles," based on old-fashioned basic ideas and options. My mission is to set you free from clutter. If the end result is "House Beautiful," great! However, being free from clutter really means "Home Sweet Home."

Along the way, I'll mention items that you can use, or purchase, to help in the process of organizing.

Before you buy anything, really think about whether it'll help. The items may be inexpensive, but buying items you don't need can get very costly. Plus, you'll be adding to the clutter! If you do buy something that you believe will work, save your receipts. You never know!

I really dislike and almost fear taking things back, but when something doesn't work, it doesn't work. I just have to grit my teeth and take it back. Sort of like jumping into a cold swimming pool!

Look at the following points about buying products:

POINTS TO PONDER

• Don't buy anything or use anything that's helping you to be a "Clutter Starter."

• Stop looking past what's causing the problem and take a good hard look at it.

• If you feel frustration every time you use an item, then there's something wrong with the item, how you're using it, or where it's located.

CAUTION

A product that works great for someone else doesn't always mean it'll work for you. When we finish our journey, you'll be able to start depending on your own buying judgement!

When we finish with the basics of your home (house, apartment, condo, townhouse, or room), and how to handle the kids' stuff, we'll then tackle the dreaded paper (mail, newspapers, magazines, newsletters, etc.).

I've offered some time management for busy people in addition to space planning and decorating tips in many of the chapters. When you daily live with challenging issues – Attention Deficit Disorder (as I do), dyslexia, learning disabilities, compulsive collecting and saving issues, or are in a wheelchair – you need simple solutions to big problems. The tips and ideas are here to help. Maybe it'll get you to think of even better ones.

So, if your windows are a little "cloudy," let's change that and shine them up!

By the way, change can almost physically hurt, so don't do all of this in one day. Take an hour or two each time you want to proceed. You'll enjoy it more and you can then get used to the change gradually.

Slowly, but steadily, you can succeed! This book to help you took me a loooonnnng time to finish writing and editing. I could only work in one or two-hour spurts, but it did get done. The evidence is before your eyes!

Please don't faint before we even start! Smile, and take along a cool drink. You CAN get through this. Have faith!

Now, let's get started to "set thine house in order!"

CHAPTER ONE

This is Sanctuary?

A Look at Your Home

Your home is meant to be your sanctuary. The place you come to when the world has beaten you down and you need to recharge your batteries. Where you can cry in private and scream out at the cruel world. But, how can you look forward to coming home when even you don't find it inviting and when your "sanctuary" itself makes you want to scream?

Inviting means warm, open and clutter-free. Let's explore what this means and how to get there from here. Take a deep breath and get ready to live your dream!

To become clutter-free, let's first look at a real life problem with abundance:

Real Estate agents sometimes face clients who have too many items lying around their homes. It could be clutter, or just too much of too many things. They may have a difficult time explaining what needs to be done to get the house sold – usually because they don't wish to offend a potential client by telling them to get rid of their stuff or to clear their counters and have a fresh clean smell in their kitchens.

Realtors believe that a look of spaciousness is more appealing to a potential buyer than a look of clutter and that this spaciousness is what helps sell a home. The smell of fresh baked cookies and soft music is also used to "complete the picture."

If a look of spaciousness is what sells a home, then let's have that look while we live in our home! Even if we don't own a home, we can still have our living spaces warm and inviting. And maybe with cookies and music, too!

The best part of being clutter-free is that even when your house needs dusting and your floors need scrubbing, it's less noticeable. When you see the clutter, the dirt and dust are more noticeable.

Let's start creating this wonderful haven of serene grace ...we'll travel almost everywhere in your home, from the front door to the back. Be assured, this place you are imagining is not just for your guests to enjoy. It's for you to enjoy – daily.

Let's walk to your front door ...pretend you're a guest visiting for the first time.

Ready or Not – The Front Door Frontier

You and I are at your front door. We've already been attacked by the numerous cobwebs grabbing at our hair and fighting to get in our mouths. It's like crawling across the desert with no water. You reach out and open the door. We walk into your living space.

- What do you see? Do you want me to see it?

- What do you hear? Do you want me to hear it?

- What do you smell? Do you want me to smell it?

- How do you feel about this space we've just entered?

- Do you want to be here, or do you want to run away?

- And are these the impressions that you want to give people visiting your home?

What am I getting at? Just this – organizing is more than finding "homes" for the stuff we own. A home for our stuff means that something has a place, and when it's not there you immediately notice its absence.

Yes, I believe all homeless items need homes, but it doesn't end there. It's also "the art of creating clutter free living spaces that are pleasing" to our guests and, more importantly, to us – a serene place where you love to be.

How can we accomplish this "house of serenity?" The dictionary describes serenity as "unclouded and bright." The "bright windows to your soul" can be your House of Serenity!

To create the art of creating clutter free living spaces that are pleasing, the how-to's are few:

- Have no cobwebs
- Have no odors that knock people over, and
- Have a room that says, "come on in and sit down."

Question: Have you ever been in those homes where you were afraid to sit down for fear of spoiling the perfection, as opposed to being afraid to sit down for fear of the dreaded swamp fever?

Answer: Of course – to both questions!

I'm not talking about creating perfection here. I only want to help you create a place that's clutter free and where you want to be. Let's look at two different scenes of "order:"

Scene 1

The door's difficult to open because the kids dumped their school books and shoes right at the front door, but you manage to shove your way in. Discarded clothing is littered from the front door to a bedroom down the hall.

As you make your way into the kitchen with the groceries you nearly stumble over a rolled up newspaper on the floor. You're wondering, "Is it today's or last week's?" You put the groceries on the floor because your kitchen counters are smeared with peanut butter and jelly from half-eaten sandwiches. And your spouse's briefcase is on the smeared jelly! And what is that horrible smell? Eeeeeeewwwwww!

You wander through the house looking for aid with the groceries and notice there's not one room, chair, couch or floor area that doesn't have "stuff" on it. You suddenly feel your stomach tighten and the tears well up, threatening to break loose. You want to Screeeeaaaam !!!

Scene 2

You open the door, walk into the kitchen and put the groceries on the kitchen counter. Aaah, something smells good! Your spouse beat you home and started dinner. The kids are working on their homework at the kitchen table. They join you and help to put the groceries away.

You notice the snack dishes have been rinsed and are in the sink. You also see the kids' shoes in the basket at the front door and the newspapers in the magazine rack. Your spouse's briefcase is nowhere in sight.

You sit down with your family and talk about the day for a few minutes and then you go to put the finishing touches on the dinner that was started. You decide to get out of your suit and go to your bedroom to change. You see a vase full of fresh flowers from the garden sitting on your dresser. You're so happy to be home!

While every home isn't filled with a spouse and kids, I hope that you get the idea. A long day is even longer when you live in the chaos of Scene 1.

When you're the one who's created the mess, you start to feel like a failure or like you're totally incapable of taking care of yourself. This leads to stress and can eventually harm your health.

Just because we may have "life challenges" to live with, we don't have to let the challenges keep us from doing what we want to do, including getting organized! And we don't have to have an outside job to make getting organized any less important. Are you ready to go for it?

I'm glad to see that you've decided to continue in your quest for bright windows! Now that we've gotten through the front door, let's journey into the foyer (entry) area.

Useless Little Area

The foyer is that seemingly useless little area that serves as an entry into the living room. There are many people who totally ignore this little space, which is really very important to your living room.

Apartments don't usually have foyers, maybe a short hall, if anything. In areas where the weather's particularly cold or snowy, the foyer used to be the area between an outside storm door and the door leading into the house.

In the Midwest and the East these areas are some-times called mud rooms. Many older homes still have these entrances. They are a great place to take off snowshoes and rain boots. There are even homes that have both the storm door entrance as well as a foyer.

In homes with a foyer, try to get the most out of this space as possible:

- A mirror on one wall, with a tall plant on the other, will visually widen this area and give it more appeal. The mirror's also useful for checking your appearance when leaving or when someone comes to the door.

- A narrow table can be used to hold mail, keys, or items that need to be taken with you when you leave.

- A standing coat pole or wall pegs can be placed here for coats and hats.

- Choice family photos can also be hung in this area.

- If you have children, you can put plastic cubbies that have a "lip" at the bottom of them in the foyer for their books and belongings.

These cubbies stack and are fairly sturdy. I recommend the cubbies with a lip so that items tossed in won't hang or roll out.

Cubbies are sold in grocery stores as vegetable bins and can also be found at variety stores, like Target.

This idea works well if the foyer door is the one that is used to enter and leave your home. If everyone uses a back door, then the cubbies are more useful in that area.

If plastic cubbies turn you off, check into Ikea, Pier Import, or furniture stores that carry bins that are serviceable and yet attractive. Etigerres with drawers are nice looking and the stuff you put in them isn't visible for others to see.

Arlyne

Arlyne couldn't afford to buy cubbies, or anything else to put at the front door for herself, her husband or her kids. But that didn't deter her. She actually found some large construction nails on one of her walks and put them in the wall behind the front door. Her kids hung their backpacks there, she hung her purse there and her husband even hung his fanny pack there. She did what she had to do to make things work. She plans on getting some nice hooks when her budget allows it.

Summary

- Create a welcoming image at your front door.
- Create a look of spaciousness by removing extra furnishings.
- Your home is not just for your guests to enjoy. It's for you to enjoy – daily.
- Organizing is the art of creating clutter free living spaces that are pleasing.
- A long day is even longer when you live in chaos.
- In homes with a foyer, try to get the most out of this space as possible.

Well, we've talked about it, walked through it and now it's time to put your will where your mouth is – so repeat the following, out loud:

I Will:

- create a warm welcome at my front door and into my foyer.
- remove furniture that is no longer useful or wise to keep.
- enjoy my home by treating myself as a guest.
- create a living space that is pleasing to myself and others.
- not make my day longer by living in chaos.

It is written that "A man's life consists not in the abundance of the things which he possesses." (Luke 12:15)

Wow, we got through the front door and the foyer – high five! It's now time to take a swig of water, mop our brow and travel to your living room.

SMILE! I see that grimace!

Come on ...you CAN do it!

OK, repeat after me: I WILL GET ORGANIZED – because I can!

CHAPTER TWO

It's Alive, It's Alive!

A Look at Your Living Room

Does anyone really "live" in their living room? Usually the only thing alive – and breeding overnight – is stuff. When a family room's available, the living room becomes a place where either stuff is put to be taken care of "later," or where guests are entertained so you won't allow anyone else in it!

Personally, I think this room should be called the front room. It's almost always at the front of the house, just beyond the front door, or at least close to it. In previous times it was called the front room. I don't know when that changed, but I'll bet my Victorian sisters of long ago were annoyed when they stopped using the term "best room." But then, maybe not because then they didn't have to keep it looking like a "best room!"

Since the living room's usually the first room seen when someone enters your home, let's get it to reflect who you are and what you're like. For instance . . .

Walking into a room that's painted bright red will reflect a totally different image of you than if the room were painted a pale blue. Neither color is right or wrong, but each gives an impression of who you are, just like walking into a room that is cluttered, or free of clutter.

If you're wondering how to create a great living room to reflect who you really are, follow me! Don't forget your water – we ARE on a long journey!

Where to Start

First, imagine what you'd like your living room to look like. Wow! Good thought! And guess what? You can really get there from here – with some planning, which I'll discuss with you throughout the book.

Second, along with planning, there are "tools" you'll need in order to clear out items not in your future vision. These tools are:

1. empty boxes, or garbage bags if you prefer (you'll need some for each room);

2. large trash cans; and

3. a marking pen to label your boxes. If you're using trash bags, tape notepaper to the bags for labeling.

Stay focused in the living room for now, and try not to leave the room while you're working here. Some hints to help you stay in this room are:

- If you see shoes or anything else that belong to your kids, spouse, or roommate, don't take them to their room! (See following paragraphs on what to do with this stuff.)

- If possible, let someone else watch your kids while you're devoting your energies to making your dream come true.

- If that's not possible, have the kids help you.

- Unless your children are babies, this de-cluttering can actually help them. You'll be training them in how to care for their belongings.

Allow yourself two hours at a time to work on this room.

Even if you're not through after two hours, stop. You'll be eager to continue if you do it slowly. This clearing process can take some time and I don't want you to get overwhelmed before you even make a small dent in the clutter. It's much better to have changes occur slowly so that it's not a shock to your emotions, or anyone else's.

Belinda

Belinda's an all or nothing gal. She's compulsive and bound and determined to have a "perfect" living/dining room for Thanksgiving, which is just a few weeks away.

There are stacks and stacks of mail, paper clippings, cartoons, articles and various clothing items around the room. My suggestion to take just an hour or two and gather one type of item at a time didn't sit well. She HAD to do it all, and in just one day. She could only afford to have me there for two hours so I tried as much as possible to have her gather like items together.

She called me the next day to say that she got the room cleared and would wait until after New Year's to start on the other rooms. When I asked her what she did with all of the stuff, she said that she became so overwhelmed at the end of the day that she shoved the rest of the stuff under her bed and in any empty cupboard, cabinet or closet space that she could find!

If you can't tolerate the thought of leaving the room incomplete after the two hours, and you have lots of clutter, ask a trusted friend to help you. Why trusted? Friends can sometimes pass judgement, or tell others your problem with clutter. And they can also get bored with helping you when they have so many other things to do. So what do you do? The best suggestion I can offer, of course, is to hire a Professional Organizer! Why? Because:

1. They're experts;

2. They're ethically bound to not divulge any information about you or your belongings; and

3. You're paying them to not get bored!

But, you're reading this book, so either you truly feel you can't afford an organizer, or you're determined that you can do it yourself. In either case, let's continue to see what we can do.

How to Get There

The following steps will help to guide you while de-cluttering. You can follow these steps for each room that's cluttered, or you can follow options that I suggest for other rooms as we travel through your home (which means that you'll have to read the entire book before you start):

1. Pick up all the papers you find in this room and put them in a box, boxes, or bags. Label the container(s) with the word "papers."

2. If you find bills, that haven't yet been paid, do NOT put them in the boxes. Find a safe place to put them until you can pay them. (Papers/bills are dealt with in another chapter.)

3. Put magazines/newspapers in their own box and label it "newspapers/magazines."

4. Pick up all the clean clothes hanging around, carefully fold them and put them into a box, boxes, or bags, labeling them "clean clothes." (When you're through working for today, put these clothes where they belong so you don't have to put them with the dirty ones again.)

5. Pick up all those smelly dirty clothes and put them in a box, boxes or bags labeled "laundry," (or stinky clothes!). When you're through in this room, put them in the hamper, or near your washing machine.

6. Pick up all items that belong in other rooms (whatever it may be) and put them in a box, boxes or bags. Label the container "belongs elsewhere."

7. Put things you want to give away into a box, boxes or bags. Label the container "give away."

8. Put the garbage (the left-over pizza, peanut butter and jelly sandwiches, etc.) into the trash can.

You can put all these things in piles on the floor if you don't have much of a mess. It's just easier putting them in boxes in order to move them to where you want them to go and it's less overwhelming.

If two hours seems like an eternity, then just clear one small section for an hour. If an hour is too much, try one-half hour. Any start is better than none. Maybe tomorrow you'll be able to spend more time. Pay attention to how you feel. Also watch that you don't forget to take your medicine and to eat before you start. Being hungry and draggy isn't helpful.

After you've picked up and separated everything you'll probably have a number of filled boxes or bags. For right now, line them up against a living room wall, out of the flow of traffic. If possible, place them so they're not in direct sight of the front door!

When the other rooms are taken care of, then we can come back and take care of these containers. The purpose right now is to give you some **Immediate Visual Calm**.

Or if you prefer, you can deal with these containers after you clear each room.

CAUTION

One of the problems with dealing with the container right away is that you may not have the space to put these items away until the room the items belong in has also been cleared of clutter. But if it makes you feel better to do so, then by all means do it. It's up to you and what you can tolerate.

Now, some questions to help that vision in your head. NO – not a test!

- Is your living room a place where people listen to music, or read?
- Do you have a piano in this room?
- Do you listen, or would like to listen, to a stereo in this room?
- Do you have or play musical instruments in this room?
- Do you have a collection of figurines in this room?
- Do you have books you would like to read in this room?
- Do you have antique pieces of furniture in this room?
- Do you have Persian rugs in this room?
- Is this a room where you want guests to gather, but not your family?

By answering these type of questions, you'll start to get ideas of what you want this room to look like, and how you want to use it.

Let's first discuss your entertainment area and then we'll proceed with the other items you may have in this room.

Entertainment Area

There are many objects in this room and we will look at them all separately.

Phonograph Records

If you still have disk phonograph recordings (records), then we'll need to find storage for these.

Carly

Carly had received some old family phonograph records and sheet music after her parents died that had been her great-grandparents. Without thinking, or going through the cardboard boxes, she stored them in her garage until she could go through them. She lived near the ocean, so her garage was pretty damp and humid. When we were clearing her garage and opened the boxes, she was horrified to find that the records had become warped (they had been stacked on top of each other inside the boxes), and the sheet music was either yellowed or crumbling to pieces. She basically lost the whole collection.

CAUTION

Disk phonograph records should be stored on their edges, preferably in a record jacket. Otherwise, cut cardboard to size and place between the records. Better still, make a jacket out of cardboard pieces, holding the pieces together with scotch tape.

If you must store phonograph records in your garage, use heavy plastic bins with tight fitting lids. If you live in a very hot and/or humid climate try to find a different storage area than the garage, basement or attic for these items, especially if you're thinking of selling the records. Also look for anti-humidity items that can be put inside the containers to pull out the moisture. Even in very dry climates, storing records and sheet music in a garage isn't the best thing to do.

Audio Cassettes

These cassettes can be stored in:

- boxes with lids that are available at office supply stores;
- shoe boxes;
- special plastic boxes made specifically to hold these cassettes;
- frames with slots, made out of cardboard, plastic or metal and are available at music stores or in audio cassette catalogs.

Put these cassettes in categories so they're easier for you to find quickly. Try using different colored labels for your different categories to help you find the cassette you want.

These audio tapes should be rewound so only their leaders show, avoiding damage to the magnetic tape. (The leader is the clear part of the tape just before the brown color starts.)

Compact Disks (CDs)

As with audiocassettes, there are also small cases specifically designed for CDs. They usually stack vertically. If you don't wish to spend the money for these cases, then you can use a shoebox, or similar type of small box.

If you're going to use a shoebox or other small box, stand the CDs on end so that the label shows.

Again, for your ease, categorize them either alphabetically, by composer, or by musical group.

Or, color code for easy identification.

CAUTION

A problem with using shoeboxes is that if you have many CDs and want to stack the shoe boxes on top of each other vertically, it makes it difficult to get the one or two CDs you want to play.

To help with this a little, try labeling the outside of the shoebox. If you keep certain composers, groups, or categories all together in one box it will help in at least finding the box you want. Then within the box you'll have to decide if it's worth your time to go alphabetical by title, composer or group.

If you know, in your heart of hearts, that you'll be pulling, shoving and throwing these shoe boxes around when wanting a CD – and you'll probably not re-stack them – then don't use them.

Picture yourself using the shoeboxes then imagine using a vertical cabinet instead where you can easily pull out just one CD without disturbing the rest.

POINT TO PONDER

Always try to picture yourself using something before you actually buy it. Don't buy it just because it sounds like a good idea – your neighbor uses it – or you read about it.

Depending on your budget, there are numerous cabinets of all sizes that will house any type of item that you want to keep. Be aware of your space availability when making these choices.

In small rooms, it's best to go vertical. If you have large rooms with a good deal of space, then cabinets are warranted. Also, the variety of cabinets is improving so that they can blend with your present furnishings to keep the look you like.

Video Cassette Tapes

If the television's in the living room and you use a VCR, then the video cassettes you collect are best stored in the same room. If you have televisions in other rooms, also with VCRs then you have the option of storing in those rooms.

Sometimes "adult" movies are in one room and "kiddie" movies are in another. So let's look at some storage places...

Bookcases will house videos without any problem. There are also video cabinets that will let you put the television on top and house the videos inside.

If you use bookcases, be sure that the shelves are just deep enough for the videos. Why? Well, if you have space in front of your videos, it's simply too easy to put something on the shelf in front of them. Then, guess what? The next time you pull out a video, off comes the item in front. And where do you think it goes? That's right, On The Floor! (And the floor is not an option!) Or, some other place where it will be left and ignored. Warning sign! This is called Clutter Start!

If you prefer not to have your videos on bookshelves, then you can put them into drawers, with the labels up so you can see them and retrieve them easily.

Don't forget to categorize them for easy access if you have quite a collection. Some possible categories are: juvenile, adventure, drama, comedy, religious, practical, musicals, documentary. You can use heavy paper stock or cut up file folders for dividers. The best way to categorize them would be to have separate drawers for each category.

"Drawers" can be filing cabinets, rolling or stationary plastic drawer units, or a more expensive wicker type unit which is actually an etagere (shelving unit) with drawers.

Money a big concern?

You can always use:

- cardboard boxes that are cut down to just beneath the top of your videos;
- or, make some shelves using old bricks, which can be painted for a dressier look, and inexpensive sheets of wood, which can also be painted or stained.

Instructions for brick bookcases

Stack two bricks on the floor under each end of one board. Also place a supporting stack of bricks every 30 inches under the board for support.

On top of that piece of wood, and directly above the bricks beneath, layer more bricks. Don't forget the supporting brick so the shelves don't sag. The height of the stack of bricks used will depend on how much of a gap you will need to slide the video out of the shelf. Just like a bookcase, you need to be able to pull the video out. Add another board on top of the brick stacks, then more bricks, a board, and so on.

You can have a floor to ceiling unit, if you wish. Don't forget to categorize! Just think how easy it will be to find what you want to watch. You will also automatically see when a tape is not "home." Everything will

soon have a home – a special place all it's own.

Oh yes, what are you going to do when a tape isn't "home?" Well, give them time out! (Put them in a corner until they behave!) (Parent Humor)

Musical Instruments

If your living room is where you'll be enjoying music, it's easier to have everything for that purpose in this room. For instance, piano, violin, clarinet, sheet music, etc.

Let's talk about these musical pieces and what to do with them.

Musical instruments need special care because of their delicate nature and value. It's best if they're in their own cases, or at the very least, covered and placed in a safe area where people won't bump into them.

Shelves or stands can be brought into the living room to hold these instruments. However, closets can also be used to store these items, if they're not in constant use.

If you're lucky enough to have some large antique pieces, you can store your musical instruments in them. And tall furniture pieces, like armoires, can house many items.

POINT TO PONDER

If you're keeping an instrument just for memory's sake, love it by encasing it in a specially made craft, shadow box, or acrylic box and hang it on a wall, or put it in a display case (like a curio cabinet). My husband was astonished when I did this with his boyhood clarinet. I also encased a picture of him with his father when they had both played the clarinet together. It's a nice memory.

Sheet Music

When you play in a band or choir, you probably have to deal with lots of sheet music. Even if you play the piano, you've probably got too much sheet music to store in the piano bench, so:

- have a pretty basket or open container to hold the sheet music;
- use bookends on top of a studio piano (wall hugger piano);
- use a clear acrylic case (the ones they make to hold magazines);
- use the clear drawers that are like a small filing cabinet and have wheels.

If you have a baby grand piano, then try a decorative container (wicker, brass, porcelain basket, etc.) for the sheet music. This can either sit on the piano, or preferably, on the floor. If you're a serious pianist, the top of the piano wouldn't work very well as every time you opened the piano lid – plop! There goes all the sheet music on the floor. Warning! This is called Clutter Start!

When you have much more than a basket-full of sheet music, a filing cabinet might be the thing to use. An antique or wooden piece would look better in the living room.

If money is not an issue, there are beautiful wooden and wicker shelving units with drawers that can be used for storage. These can be found at furniture stores and through catalogs. Try to find one with drawers high enough so you can stand your sheet music upright.

Or get a wood or metal bookcase (new or used) whose shelves are just deep enough to hold the sheet music upright.

You can lay them down on the bookshelf, and in the drawers, but remember that you'll have to lift papers to get to the sheet you want. This is another temptation for **Clutter Start!**

In either case, it would help if you tried to sort your music alphabetically, by title category (music type), or Composer.

However, how do you do that when you're using something other than a filing cabinet, like a bookcase? Let's explore that.

The simplest way to use a bookcase for sheet music is to take a colored piece of thick paper, or a colored file folder (which you can cut in half to have two single pieces), and put it in between your alphabetical or category separations, making sure it shows above the sheet music. (This will also work in your file cabinets if you aren't using Pendaflexes to separate your categories, or composers.)

If the sheet music is too tall for the file folder or colored paper, you could even try what they do in Doctor's offices: Take the file folder, or heavy paper, and lay it on its long side, separating your sheets of music by your chosen categories (alphabet, composer, group); label the end that sticks out beyond the shelf. Hopefully the file folder doesn't stick out too much beyond the edge of the shelf. If it does, try cutting it back a little before you label it.

If you have the type of dyslexia that has you confusing letters, then maybe different colored pieces of paper will help you find your category faster. Color also works well for those with ADD and gives a quick visual as to where the sheet music is that you're searching for.

Labeling the shelves is another help if color disturbs you, or you're color-blind. It would still help to use some type of separation between categories.

Antique pieces of furniture may also work well in containing sheet music, and they would look especially nice next to a baby grand piano. Some antique book cases have glass doors on them (barrister bookcases). This helps keep the dust off your collection and also keeps the sheets from fluttering to the floor when someone walks by. Of course, if you're bookshelves are crammed with sheet music, that probably won't happen anyway!

You can also store the sheet music in plastic envelopes found in office supply stores. Most of them come in different colors and sizes, so you should be able to find something that you like.

These envelopes are also see-through, which helps those of us with ADD. You can then put these envelopes on your bookcases, or in drawers. Remember to label the outside of the envelope so you don't have to wonder what type of music's inside.

Now that we've looked at your options for your music, let's look at other items that you're storing in the living room.

Books

Sometimes living rooms are quiet areas where reading is done, possibly while listening to music. Some soft lighting, possibly with pink bulbs, can make this a very soothing room.

Dimmer switches on the lighting fixtures can add to this feeling of comfort. However, good strong lighting is necessary on the actual reading matter. So, a variety of lighting is needed. But we also have to find places to keep the books we want to read here.

Books seem to have a life of their own. Some are rare and others are quite common. It doesn't really matter, as long as you have space for them.

Denise

Denise loves books, the more the better. Because of her Obsessive Compulsive Disorder (OCD) problems, she counts each and every one, whether adding to or deleting (rarely) from her collection. She lives in a small home and keeps her books in bookcases in her bedroom, all 500 of them! This gives her easy access to whatever she wants to read. The problem is, she doesn't. The books are for looks. Because of her OCD and ADD problems, she has never felt very smart and her books are used to tell others that she's not as dumb as she feels.

"The proud and arrogant man, 'Mocker' is his name; he behaves with overweening pride." Proverbs 21:24.

If you're really keeping the books to show off (come on now, be honest), then donate them immediately and rid yourself of the clutter, the feelings of deceit and the upkeep headaches. Libraries will take the books, as will some schools. The real test is: Do you read them? If you do, then let's get those books into good storage homes.

The only other reason for keeping a largely unread pile of books is to give them to your children, or their children. Consider letting them have those books while they're rearing their own families. Keeping a "library" active is the whole purpose of books!

Evie's Idea

Evie and her husband designed a wall-to-wall, floor-to-ceiling bookcase, with a sliding ladder. It reminded me of law libraries I had been in. It's absolutely beautiful. They did have hundreds of books and so used a useless wall with a cathedral ceiling on which to build the bookcase.

This was an expensive project, and you don't need to build such an elaborate unit. If you have "hundreds of books," you can connect bookcases to each other and create your own wall unit.

If you anchor the cases to the wall, it's even possible to stack them, creating your own wall-to-wall, ceiling-to-floor masterpiece. Of course, you too will then have to use a ladder to reach the upper shelves.

Another option takes some carpentry knowledge. The inside of your walls are made up of vertical 2" x 4" wood separations, or 4" x 6"s, depending on the structure. If you break through the wall, the space is perfect for paperbacks to fit in, once you add shelves between the columns.

Instructions

Cut some wood to fit the width of the spaces between the 2" x 4"s and you have a "built-in" bookcase. Paint the interior to match your wall coloring and it looks as though it were originally made that way.

If you're short on money, then you can build yourself a bookcase, using the bricks and plywood sheets described for storing videotapes. Be sure to use sturdier wood as books are quite heavy. Flimsy, thin boards will sag, causing the whole unit to fall.

As with your music, videos and recordings, categorize your books so that you can easily find the book you want to read. This will also make it easier for others to find a book to read, or to marvel at your collection! The ones you really read!

Some common categories of books are: fiction, history, geography, religion, science, how-to-do-it, crafts, biography, self-help, humor, art, and reference.

Keep all your books in one location (except cookbooks that are best kept in the kitchen, or business books, best in the office). When a book is not at "home," you now know what to do! Yep, straight to the corner!

Other items to think about in your living room are the furniture, collectibles, window coverings, pictures, mirrors and wall hangings. There are different ways to address all these items. You can walk in and say, "Hello, Mr. Mirror," or, "Good morning, Miss Knick Knack." Just kidding! When I say address, what I mean is, what are you going to do with all that stuff?

Collectibles

Let's say that you have collectibles "coming out of your ears," and you're displaying all of them, everywhere, including the kitchen and bathroom. Take a good look at these items, and all the rest of your collectibles.

Can you see each collectible and appreciate the beauty of each piece, or are they so crowded on a shelf, counter, or bookcase that they are figuratively "lost"?

Fran

Fran has approximately 300 Hummel figurines, which are small, childlike statues. Some of the pieces are quite valuable. Because she has so many of them, they are crowded into the living room and elsewhere, making it difficult to appreciate them because you really can't look at just one without seeing all the others, too. To look at all of these the minute you walk in is overwhelming.

If your collections resemble this scene, lessen the visual impact. You can "gift" them to children or grandchildren for birthdays or holidays, or to a favorite friend or other relative.

"Sell your possessions...you will have treasure in heaven."
(Matthew 19:21)

Okay. I know that most of you would rather die than get rid of these cute little items you've collected, so let's see how we can show them off.

Keep only three pieces in any one area to allow full viewing of each piece. If you have no other place to put the extra items, then carefully store them for six months, or a year.

What? Store my precious Hummels, Lladros, etc.? Never! OK, then you're saying that you want to suffer with being visually overwhelmed and endure all the cleaning you need to do. And if you have a cleaning lady, don't blame her when she breaks one of these items because there's just too many to work around.

There are two hidden advantages to featuring a few of your collectibles at a time:

- You and others will start appreciating each piece for its beauty instead of their being lost in a sea of similar items. You'll be treating your collection in the same way great museums do. They have great storehouses of items from which they pull only a few items for public viewing which are rotated with others periodically.

- When you have a few good items on display, you'll be handling them again and again, able to enjoy their beauty and value. Maybe that's why you started collecting them in the first place. The alternative is to let them all just sit and collect dust.

Chosen to store those extra items? Good for you! The best storage, again, will be plastic bins with tight fitting lids. Be sure to cushion the bottom, sides and top of the bin with bubble wrap, newspapers, tissue paper, paper towels, paper sacks, or plastic sacks.

Store the bins on closet shelves or floors, under stairwells, in the garage, basement or attic. The closer the storage area is to you, the easier it will be to change out your current display with your stored items.

Now we come to an additional cluttering ordeal for your living room, and other rooms, the holidays. Sorry, but you may as well look at it now, hopefully BEFORE the holidays.

Holidays offer decorating delights, or trauma, whichever defines your state of mind. Let's talk about the holidays and all our stuff for them.

When you have a huge collection of Christmas decorations, where are you going to display them? You already have every shelf, bookcase, counter top and table filled with other things. We won't even talk about the chairs and the floor!

If you want to display all your Christmas items, then do so. Oh, oh, what's the catch, what's she going to tell me now? (I know you're still smarting from my telling you to store too many of your collectibles.) The catch is, you need to find space for all of it! And that's stressful! What can you do?

Well, remove and store some or all of your daily decorative items until after Christmas, or Halloween, or Easter, or Chanukah, or whatever other holiday season you're decorating for.

Imagine this: you have a beautiful and valuable porcelain figurine on your coffee table. Now it's the holidays. You have a beautiful, valuable porcelain Christmas angel that would be perfect for the coffee table. You put both items on the table, side-by-side, right? Nope!

The non-holiday item is there all year for everyone to admire. The holiday item is seen only on the holiday, so why take away from its beauty by making it compete for attention?

However, a decorator friend said that three is perfect for decorating. She groups anything in threes, if they're similar (books, plants, figurines, etc). Even my gardener planted three like items in our yard.

If you have holiday items that would look good together, go ahead and display three of them. Either store the non-holiday item, or move it to a temporary place until after the holiday. Now... picture your holiday scene! If done with just your holiday decorations, your home will look like you've stepped into another time or place. Just think how delightful this can look to old and young alike.

True, you have to have time to put up and take down all this stuff. But, It's All Your Stuff That You Want to Keep, so enjoy!

If you're going to keep it all, use it! Let your entire home reflect the holiday. The boxes you emptied of these treasures can be used for the non-holiday items you need to store for a while. Thereafter, delight in whatever holiday you're celebrating, let it fill all senses of sight, sound and smell, without any conflicts from your non-holiday delights.

Let's move on and talk about your windows and what to do with them. Yes, you open and close them, but are they naked?

Window Coverings

The above seasonal and holiday ideas can also apply to periodically changing window coverings and furniture. For example, if you have very little money and want a sunshine affect at your windows, try some inexpensive sheets. No, I don't mean to cover up the window itself.

Try winding a sheet around a curtain rod at the top of the window in a valence affect and hang a sheet at each side of the window that you can tie back with a cord. If your living room windows require privacy, you can put up a tension rod and hang sheer or opaque curtains from it to match the sheet's colors.

If you can afford to buy ready-made curtains or drapes, or have them made, follow the same thought. Have sunshine and flower type curtains for the winter and winter scene, or cool colored curtains for the summer.

On your couches and chairs drape blanket throws, or use pillows of the same color in the curtains or drapes. Arrange silk flowers of the same coloring to follow the theme. We change our clothes with the seasons, so why not our homes?

Let's now take a look at your furniture, the good, the bad, and the ugly.

Furniture

Too much furniture in a room can also create visual clutter. Keep the best pieces and find someone who can really use the ones that you can do without. There are many organizations that desperately need furniture. Halfway houses and women's shelters are always looking for furniture and they don't care if the furniture isn't brand new. But obviously, they can't use junk anymore than you can.

Be careful about the placement of your furniture. If you have a really large room, an intimate setting with scattered side chairs might work best. A small room might look better with furniture pieces not too close to each other, giving a more open look.

End tables can hold a table lamp, interesting books (only 3 please), a knick knack or a candy jar, depending on the size of your table. Large items make your table look smaller and smaller items make the table look larger.

Placement of end tables and coffee tables is also important. For safety's sake, these tables should be placed where the probability of someone bumping into them is low. And don't be afraid to get out of the let's-line-up-all-the-furniture-along-the-walls routine. If your room is home to a baby grand piano, or file cabinets, or many pieces of furniture, be sure to place them to allow easy movement around them and through the room.

Example of line-up-all-the furniture-along-the-walls: My living room is a typically small one, with a dining room off to the side of it. When you walk in the front door you enter the foyer area (that useless space) and see the fireplace straight ahead in the living room.

To the left, against the wall, I had my couch — stereo on one side — end table at the other, all lined up with the wall. In front of the couch was the coffee table and on the other side of the coffee table, on the right as you're looking in, was my loveseat (fancy word for short couch). To the right of the loveseat is my dining room.

So, when you walked in and saw the fireplace, you also saw three parallel lines of items (I I I) in front of the fireplace: a couch to the left, a coffee table in the middle, and a couch to the right, cutting off easy access to the dining room. Since the living room is small, this arrangement was wonderful for up to four people. When we had guests over, it was terrible.

I fretted over that living room for years. The flow of traffic was terrible, also. As an organizer it made me crazy. I then tried moving the smaller couch to the right of the larger one, at a right angle, making an "L" shape. Now when you walked in, all you saw was the back of the loveseat. Ugh! I was still unhappy.

One winter, however, brought a delightful solution. I shifted the loveseat to the right, away from the couch, to make way for the Christmas tree. Because of the way I had shoved it, it sat at an angle, in an almost out of shape V formation from the couch

But the couch was still straight.

The loveseat's back was angled to the side of my piano (which is a wall hugger), which sits on a narrow side wall. So I now had a straight line and an angled line (I........../piano). When I walked back into the room to decorate the tree, my eye caught the new angle of the loveseat. It interested me enough to angle the coffee table in front of it.

Wow! What a change! I now have room for chairs in the living room and people can even walk from my living room into my dining room without squeezing by the piano or banging into the serving table, also in the dining room. See, even organizers walk around with their eyes shut to what's right in front of them!

Enough of me – back to your furniture. Some of you get furniture from parents and grandparents after their death. This is very difficult, particularly if you have OCD. Once you've touched the furniture on your turf, it's yours! You'll need to work very hard to convince yourself that you really have no need for all the furniture. I believe that there are probably some items you can really use; but rarely does anyone have need for all of it. Discuss this out loud with yourself, with your spouse, a therapist, or a trusted friend.

If the furniture you've received are antiques, then you have the additional problem of considering their money value in addition to their emotional value. Again, talk to yourself about your need for the items. Ask yourself some of the following questions:

- Can another relative use some of the pieces?
- Is there a favorite person in my life that I would like to give something to?
- Can I sell any of the items that I really don't need?
- Can I donate the items to a nursing home, or senior center?
- Is this furniture really usable, or does it need umpteen repairs that I really can't afford?
- Am I keeping this furniture because I truly need it, have room for it and can it replace the stuff I'm going to throw out?

Sorry, tough questions, but ones you have to ask. If you're really having problems, just look at one item at a time when asking these questions. Maybe just one piece will be useful, but not the whole lot.

And beneath all of our furniture are the rugs.

Rugs

What about those lovely Persian rugs on your floor? Can you see them? Are you hiding their beauty with all the clutter, papers, magazines, etc.? Even if you have wall-to-wall carpet, are you piling clutter on top of it? Is the carpeting stained from all the newspapers you throw on the floor without even thinking?

If you're going to invest in expensive items, then enjoy them by making it possible for them to be seen. Persian rugs take special care, so check with the manufacturer about how best to preserve them. Even wall-to-wall carpeting needs a good deep cleaning yearly. You also need to check for stains constantly as they will ruin your carpet.

Our next area to look at is our walls and what we put on them.

Pictures / Photographs / Mirrors / Wall Hangings

Are you hanging photo after photo of all the relatives in your life on your living room walls? Are the photos in dime store frames?

Unless those photographs are very special, maybe in oil and framed in gold, the living room is not the best place for them. They would look better in a hall, bedroom, study, or grouped on a small round table.

Sometimes the family room is a good place for photographs, if the family room doesn't double as a living room.

If you're going to hang pictures in the living room, then arrange them in an interesting way to help widen the look of your room, or to make it appear taller, or possibly shorter than it is. This can be done by:

- placing the pictures in a horizontal line across the largest wall (to widen);
- hanging in a vertical line from near the ceiling to just above a couch or chair (to make the room appear taller);
- or hang in a square group just above a couch or chair (to make the room appear shorter).

Don't be afraid to experiment

You can also make your photos appear as though they are hanging from a satin ribbon with a bow at the top. The ribbons could match the colors of your room.

One place where people put family photos is on the piano. In some old movie scenes they show certain family photos sitting on top of the baby grand piano. Apparently the piano is never played, it's just for looks!

I wouldn't put some of my crew on top of the piano (I can hear them screaming now), but that doesn't mean it isn't a great place if it can be easily removed. A cherished child's or loved one's photo in a decorative frame would look great.

Concerning decorative pictures in the living room – depending on size and wall space – use one or several that reflects your taste and also blends with the color scheme of your room. Work with the color scheme that you now have, or change it.

Remember, the old, cluttered house is going bye-bye so maybe some of the old color schemes need to be put to rest also. What emerges needs to be the real you, what you love and what you want to look at for a long time.

Pictures can help to reflect the inner you. Mirrors in the living room can also help to lengthen or widen the look of a small room. When you use mirrors, be careful where you place them so that they reflect some-thing nice. A mirror showing a French door leading to a garden, or a group of plants, will look far better than a blank wall.

Summary

- The living room's usually the first room seen when someone enters your home – have it reflect who you are and what you're like.
- Use empty boxes, or garbage bags to gather all the stuff.
- Have available a large trash can.
- Have a marking pen to label your boxes.
- Have notepaper to tape to trash bags.
- Allow yourself two hours at a time to work on this room.

Remember: Any start is better than none

Once you have the living room cleared, promise yourself to make an honest effort to keep it that way. Try every day by taking five minutes (use a timer) to pick up items in one room. If you have children, get them to help. Even very young children can pick up items and bring them to you.

If you multiply the five minutes by the number of rooms in your house, you'll know how long it might take you to clear out the rooms, once you've organized everything.

So, if you live in a three-room apartment, 15 minutes is the most you'll need to pick up things that are lying around. A six-room apartment or home may take 30 minutes, but probably less as you get comfortable with putting things away.

Don't beat yourself up if it takes you longer at the beginning of this process. When I say to take five minutes to pick things up it's because I don't want you to feel like all you do every day is pick things up!

If you don't want to instruct you on how to dust and vacuum. But, you'll see, once things have been cleared away and put in "homes," (a place for everything), that cleaning does becomes less of a chore, whether you do it yourself or have someone else do it.

And, before you start, say to yourself:

I Will:

- decide what I'm going to use each room for;
- look for various containers to use for sheet music, including file cabinets and book cases;
- try to use book cases to hold tapes and CDs in addition to books;
- store musical instruments carefully in their own cases or in large furniture pieces;
- store extra collectible items and rotate for seasonal or holiday affect;
- display only three collectibles or other items in any one spot;
- experiment with hanging pictures at different levels, depending on wall and room size.

Yea! We've changed your living room. It's now time to go into your family room, so remember the joy you feel with your new living room and that your family room is next!

What? Tired? OK, we can rest for now. You did a great job on the living room! Meet ya tomorrow in the family room – and don't forget your drink and snacks.

CHAPTER THREE

Family/Rumpus/ Bonus/Clutter Room?

A Look at Your Family Room

The family room, in many cases, is really the living room turned into an all-purpose room. Many names have been given to this room, but they all amount to the same thing. A room big enough to collect all the stuff we want and a place where it doesn't matter how bad it looks ...'cause its not the living room!

Making this room work is very important since many activities may be taking place here. You may watch television or listen to the stereo here. It could also be where:

- meals are eaten,
- clothes are ironed,
- homework is done,
- clothes are folded,
- bills are paid,
- clothes are sewn,
- letters are written,
- clothes are ...well, you get the idea!

If all of these activities are taking place, the room needs to be as clutter-free as possible. But how? One person creates clutter. When you have many people in your household, an avalanche of stuff can pile up. And you know what happens in an avalanche! Let's take a closer look at this room and see how we can cope with it.

Meals

The rush of today's living has resulted in many of us eating in front of the television in order to watch the news or let the children see their favorite cartoons. Let's not even discuss the programs that our teens want to watch!

Even if you eat in front of the television, it's best that everyone eats in a calm setting. This can be helped by having a place to eat with meal items quickly available. So let's take another quiz:

- When meals are eaten in front of the television, how are the meals served?
- Does everyone get TV trays, use their laps, the floor, or a small table?
- If they use TV trays, are they conveniently stored close by for easy access and putting away? (Leaving them propped open at all times really creates a visual impact of clutter and they are easily tipped over if they're in the way.)
- If everyone uses their laps, or the floor, do you put something down on the floor so that there's less of a mess to clean up? Tablecloths or towels would be beneficial.
- If you actually eat at a small table, is it free of clutter so you can just sit down to eat?
- Do you have a small basket with napkins and condiments available, or do you run into the kitchen for everything?
- Is there a place for you to store placemats when not in use (if you use them)?

If you do eat at a table, drape it with a large tablecloth that hangs to the floor. You can then store a small basket with napkins, etc., underneath the table.

This only works, of course, if you have a table with the legs in the corners, rather than in the middle. If you do have a pedestal table, maybe a small picnic basket on the table, or on the floor near the table, would be beneficial. However, be careful about using open containers on the floor if you have pets that roam about. Cat or dog hairs on napkins aren't very appealing with meals!

Another activity we usually do in this room is ironing and sewing, unless you're me! And if you're me, who am I? Oh, dear.

Sewing/ironing

If you sew and use a portable sewing machine, it might also fit under the table. I have a portable sewing machine, but I also have a pedestal table, so putting the machine under the table just doesn't work. Since my table sits in a small side area in the family room, my machine sits in a corner by the table, covered with a small lace tablecloth. No one notices it unless they are sitting at the table.

Remember, you don't have to put everything out of sight to make a clutter-free room. It just needs to be out of traffic and easily accessible.

Many people iron their clothing every single morning, while preparing for work or school. This usually means that the ironing board stays up forever.

If you're lucky enough to have a large laundry room, it might be better to have the ironing board set up there. It's an ideal spot to iron as the activity level is low.

However, when it has to be in the family room, we have to avoid disaster. It does take up a lot of room, and if you leave the iron on it, it can easily be knocked over.

We don't want you or anyone else getting a broken toe by a falling iron, so lets try the following:

- When not in use, unplug the iron and place it beneath the ironing board (when it's cool!).
- Get double use out of the ironing board if it stays up most of the time. Place a chair next to the ironing board then lower the board to a height that you find comfortable when seated. Drape the ironing board with a vinyl tablecloth. You now have a working surface to pay bills, write letters, sew, or let the kids color.

You could even buy a piece of wood to put on the ironing board (just a little wider than its width), to make a wider desk-like work surface. You can still drape it with a vinyl tablecloth.

IRONING CHATTER
When you're ironing, have either a rolling clothes rack next to you to put your ironed clothes on, or over-the-door hangers that are within easy reach for you to put the clothes on.

Paying Bills

More and more people are opening their mail and paying bills while seated in their comfy recliner. Don't feel guilty about this. It really doesn't matter where the bills get paid – as long as they get paid!

To make this process easier on you, try the following:

- buy an inexpensive lap tray to write on;
- put your bills in a basket alongside your recliner. In the basket keep pens, envelopes, scotch tape, a small stapler, staple remover, scissors and postage stamps – there you go, your own instant office;
- and have a wastebasket close by.

If you want to keep all your mail by the recliner, then try a picnic basket. It's wide enough for lots of mail and office supplies, yet can be closed to keep things looking tidy.

WARNING!!
Don't keep shoving mail into your basket or you'll have clutter start. This is just a temporary mail home and quickie office. (Check out how to handle your paperwork in the "papers" chapter.)

Glenda

Glenda was pooped when she came home at night and, being single, had the luxury of kicking off her shoes, popping a TV dinner in the microwave, or eating a take-out dinner. She liked to just sink into her easy chair and forget everything. She was, however, concerned that her bills were paid on time and had even put a small desk in her kitchen to act as an office area.

Unfortunately, Glenda soon realized that she never used her desk and it just became a place to stack things. Since she did spend time in her easy chair unwinding, we set up a mail area next to the chair where she could hold her mail and open it when convenient. She wasn't sure if this new place would work, but agreed to try it for at least 21 days.

Glenda called me after one week. She was delighted with her new mail area and had bought a decorative small suitcase to put near the chair to hold her mail, stamps, envelopes, etc. She also bought another decorative container for the other side of the chair which held her crossword puzzles, which helped her calm down after a hard day.

So, she no longer felt guilty about "plopping" after work – and her bills were getting paid! She could truly just sit and relax for as long as she wanted.

Even if you're married with children, if you like to relax in a certain area and you tend to read your mail there, or your magazines and newspapers, then fix the area to help you do that.

Summary

- The room needs to be as clutter-free as possible.
- It's best that everyone eats in a calm setting.
- Have a place to eat and meal items quickly available.
- You don't have to put everything out of sight to make a clutter-free room.
- Make use of your ironing board.
- It really doesn't matter where the bills get paid – as long as they get paid!

Wow, we've traveled far. But you have to stay with this, so repeat the following until you believe it:

I Will:

- create a clutter free and comfortable room;
- create a place to eat that is calm and soothing;
- have everything I need to eat with in this room without running to the kitchen;
- keep things out of traffic zones so I don't fall – again;
- use my ironing board to the best of my ability;
- relax and pay my bills without stressing.

So there! See, you can do it!

Now, let's go into another area that plagues us with clutter, the dining room. I see you hiding. Come on, try it, you'll like it!

CHAPTER FOUR

Eat in My Dining Room?

A Look at Your Dining Room

Do you ever eat in your dining room, or is it just for guests on the holidays? Just for guests? Want to be your own guest? Yes – that's the attitude! Let's go!

Dining rooms are in areas of the home where there is usually a great deal of light and, therefore, makes a great place to eat.

Breakfast in a sun-filled room. Aaah! What a delight! Even if the room is darker or an interior room, it's fun to eat at the dining room table. It's big, and meals are just a bit more special than when eaten at a kitchen table.

Sometimes people use their dining room tables as worktables. For instance:

Scene 1

There are piles of papers, books, briefcases, sewing machine, laundry baskets and whatever else may fit on this long expanse of space, including the chairs and floor. There is no tablecloth of any type protecting the beautiful wood finish of the table.

Sometimes people use their dining room tables as an actual table! For instance:

Scene 2

The dining room table has a nice tablecloth on it and is set with placemats and cloth napkins in napkin rings. There are uncluttered chairs around it. The floor is clear and there are live or silk plants in the corner. China sparkles in the china cabinet.

Which dining room do you want to walk into? Let's look at handling the clutter we found in Scene 1.

How to Start

Remember how we tackled the living room and the supplies we used? We'll do the same for this room. However, because it's smaller, we're going to actually put some of the items where you really want them to go unless you'd rather wait until all rooms are done.

- Take the papers and put them in the box that you've already started a paper collection in. (We'll talk about papers in the Paper chapter);

- Take the books to your living room or family room. If you're not sure where you want to put them, then put them in a box with the news papers and magazines. We'll sort it out later;

- Put your briefcase in your office or at the front door in the container you've put there or on the table that's there for that purpose;

- Put your sewing machine in the family room, hobby room, or laun dry room. If you have no where else to put the sewing machine and this is typically where you use it, will it fit under the table? Will it be out of the way if you put it against a wall and cover it? Since we're trying to clear the dining room table you might have to get creative with storing the sewing machine. Look at putting it behind a couch or side-chair;

- Put the laundry baskets where your washer and dryer are. If you go to a laundromat or to an outside laundry room, try putting the basket(s) in a closet.

In other words, work toward that clear dining room picture in Scene2, or one that you have in mind. If you have a dining room, it's either an extension of the living room, or it's a formal room, usually next to the kitchen.

Either way, it's a place where dining should happen, not havoc. Get your family (or roommates) to help you create this peaceful eating area. Why walk into that nice living room we just got straightened out and look beyond and see that cluttered dining room?

Don't be afraid to start, but also don't expect that the "a picture perfect" room will happen in ten minutes. Change takes time, but it really can occur if you want it to. Gradual change is sometimes better for everyone, especially in shared space.

It's important, therefore, for the whole family to get into the act. If one day the dining room is a mess and the next day it's clutter free, it may take others quite a while to adjust. After all, when you get it organized, it's an open invitation to clutter it up again! But if the whole family is involved and knows how to keep the areas clutter free, because they know where things belong, change will be easier.

You may still have to insist that things be put back in order on a regular basis. But if you use a timer for just five minutes your family (or roommates) may be a bit more cooperative than if they think a job will take fifteen minutes! And if they still want their own space cluttered (their room), fine. But not in this space.

These rooms we have walked through – the foyer, the living room, the family room, the dining room – are part of the "communal living areas." They have gradually become cluttered by the efforts of those who share them. Visualize what you want for each room then gradually work toward that end.

Summary

- Clear the dining room the same way you did for the living room.
- Get everyone living in the house to help, using five-minute time slots.
- Get creative in finding places for difficult items (sewing machines).
- Strive to keep the communal living areas clear of clutter.

I Will:

- get my family to help me;
- set a timer when organizing so I don't get overwhelmed;
- try to find different storage areas for my hard to store items;
- sing – because I love this new place to eat!

Now that the dining room seems to be under your control, let's tackle another communal area, the kitchen.

"Let all things be done decently and in order." (1 Corinthians 14:40)

Again, if you're tired, rest. Eat, take your meds and dream of what you want your kitchen to look like. Gee, I'd kind of like that kitchen! Come on, let's go for it.

CHAPTER FIVE

Where's Your Heart?

A Look at Your Kitchen

The kitchen is said to be the "heart of the home." If your kitchen is a mess, how can you provide meals with a loving heart? All you want to do is get the job over with, sometimes with murder in your heart instead of love!

If you live alone, you probably don't even bother treating yourself as a special person. And you probably also opt to grab fast food instead of cooking.

Or maybe you eat your dinner over the kitchen sink. You wouldn't dream of setting the table with lace and china just for you, would you?

Okay, men, maybe not lace and china, but probably not even a table-cloth or dishes, instead of paper plates.

So, let's see what we can do about getting your kitchen to stand at attention when you walk in! When we get your kitchen and home in order, you'll see that life is less stressful because your peace at home carries through all areas of your life.

Since every home has different needs, don't feel as though you're "hopeless" if the following suggestions aren't working for you. I've listed quite a few because the kitchen has so much stuff in it. But if they don't help, try to get a little more creative. There's always a solution. Let your instincts, imagination and good sense take over. If you're really out of ideas, Email me and we'll walk through it together!

If you want to go directly to your specific problem area, the following list is what we'll cover in the kitchen:

- Counters & Related Items
- Cupboards, Upper (including walls)
- Cupboards, Lower
- Drawers
- Junk Drawer
- Refrigerator
- Tips
- Cooking – some time saving ideas

Counters & Related Items

Our first step in the kitchen is to do something about all the stuff we've gathered on our counters – large utensils, appliances, cups and mugs, the dish drainer and cleaning items.

Large Utensils

Chunky utensils (spatulas, potato mashers, large spoons) can be kept in a drawer or in a nice container on the counter.

If your counter and drawer space is limited, use a wall utensil rack. These racks are made of plastic or metal and have either pegs or hooks to hang the utensil on. If you have duplicates, keep the best one and REALLY TRY give the extra to someone who really needs it.

Appliances

To save cleaning time, appliances that are not used very often can be put in the lower cupboards, especially the larger appliances. Keeping these on the counter top adds to the visual clutter.

Also try the "space saving" appliances that attach beneath the upper cupboards.

Roll-out shelves are a great addition when you need to store items inside your cupboards. When you have heavy appliances, these shelves will save your back.

If the roll-out shelves are too expensive, find some heavy boxes that fit your cupboard. They're not as easy to use as the shelf, but you'll be able to pull it out a little way to get at what you want.

Tackling Counter Challenges

For those of you who have a hard time clearing the counter tops because you have a need to see everything, let's try the following exercise:

- Take the smallest appliance you have and put it in a cupboard. This needs to be an appliance that you don't use every day. If you use your can opener almost daily then it's not the right appliance to start with!
- When you are used to that one appliance being in the cupboard, try another.
- As soon as you get comfortable with that item being in the cup board, try another.
- Continue until all the items you're not using all the time are safely resting in their new home!

This process may take awhile, so don't think it's taking you too long. Changing habits takes some time, but if you're earnest, you'll get there! And don't listen to those naysayers who just laugh when you tell them what you're trying to do. In fact, don't tell them!

Do you know that people actually try to sabotage others when they find out you're trying to change? If you've ever smoked or drank and then quit, you'll know exactly what I'm talking about.

Cups & Mugs

Cups and mugs look great when hanging beneath the upper cupboards. If you live in earthquake country, use the safety hooks available at most hardware stores.

Cups can also be hung from very small fancy door knobs which have been attached to a wall. While this looks really attractive, they can be unsafe in earthquake country or with young kids around, so buy knobs that hold the cups securely.

Dish Drainer

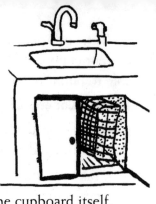

- Find a dish drainer that will fit in the sink itself if you have a two-sink basin.

- Or, store your dish drainer in the cupboard beneath the sink.

- Or, store the dish drainer on the inside of the cupboard door.

- Or, store the dish drainer on the inside wall of the cupboard itself.

Small Cleaning Items

There are sink cabinet inserts that you can install for little cleaning items. These inserts have plastic interiors and hold small cleaning items like sponges, soap pads, scrubbies, brushes, etc.; things that always create a mess on the sink when they are wet and are just one more item to pick up when you're trying to clean.

Instructions

Open the false wooden area of the sink cabinet just below the lip of the sink and just above the cupboard doors, and install a pull down compartment that you can buy from Home Depot, Home Base and other large do-it-yourself hardware stores. It's worth the trouble, so if you can't do it yourself, grab someone who can!

If installing the pull down compartments is not something you want to deal with, you can install a small wire basket to the inside door of the cupboard beneath the sink. Find a plastic container that will fit inside the basket to keep smaller items from falling out. The plastic container will also keep things from dripping inside the cabinet and can be rinsed out occasionally.

If you really don't want to install anything, find a container that allows for drainage and put all the cleaning items into it and place it somewhere on your counter that isn't in the way, or very noticeable. There are also containers with suction cups on the back of them that fit on the wall of the sink. Soap pads fits nicely into them.

Our next step is to look into our upper cupboards and see what to do with everything that's hiding up there. Oh, come on – it'll feel good, when we're done, to be able to open the doors – and not get hit in the head!

Cupboards, Upper

In this section we'll try to find space for your plates, bowls, glasses, cups and saucers. Then we'll look at your storage for packaged goods and cans.

Plates & Bowls

Gather all your plates and bowls that you use every day and try to keep them on the lowest shelf for easy access. If you're in a wheelchair, you may have to put your dishes on roll-out shelves in the lower cupboards.

Stack dinner plates all together in one stack; salad plates in one stack; and bowls in one stack. If you have the room, try to avoid stacking smaller plates or bowls on top of larger ones. This causes nothing but frustration when you're trying to get a larger plate out and have to lift all the smaller ones first!

It's better if you keep the plates and bowls near the dishwasher (if you use a dishwasher), otherwise, near your sink. This is to ease putting away.

The dishes that you don't use every day (and don't want in a china cabinet) can be put on the highest shelves (if you're tall), or in lower cupboards (if you're short or in a wheelchair).

Glasses, Cups & Saucers

Gather all your glasses, cups and saucers and also put them on a bottom shelf near the dishwasher or sink.

If you run out of room on one shelf, put your glasses and cups on the shelf above the dishes. The dishes are heavier and will be easier to pick up from the lower shelf.

In general, try to keep lighter items on the top shelves of upper cupboards and heavy breakable items on lower shelves.

It's best if items you use all the time are as close to you and where you use them as possible. In other words, try to arrange your kitchen so that you make as few repeated movements as possible.

In a very small kitchen, it doesn't matter as much about your movements because everything is basically right near you. If you keep like items together, it's a snap to turn around and grab what you want.

However, when you have a very large kitchen, or one that has an "L" shape, rather than a square shape, movement and placement of items is important. Think about the steps you take when working in your kitchen.

Example: if your refrigerator is all the way to the left at the end of a long counter and you want to make some sandwiches, then forcing yourself to take all the items near the sink at the opposite end is wasting time and energy. All you're doing is constantly walking back and forth from the refrigerator to the sink area.

Practice

Take out of the refrigerator all of the items you need to make a sandwich and place it on the counter nearest the refrigerator. Take the items that will need to be washed and cut to the sink area. When you're through washing and cutting, take them back to where the sandwich items are and make your sandwich. Where is your plate? Near enough to reach for – or should you have picked it up when you were at the sink area? Now you can put all the items back in the refrigerator with just a step or two.

This practice may sound strange to some of you, but the rest of us know that even something as simple as making lunch can cause us grief. Start paying attention to where you store items and use them so that you can make the best use of your time and space.

Let's take a look at the storage spaces you have available for your canned and boxed items.

Cupboard & Pantry Storage

Keep all boxed and packaged items together on one shelf, in groups. Example: cereal boxes all to the right on one shelf and pancake, waffle and cake mixes all to the left. Or maybe they'll all fit to the right and you can then put rice and pasta items to the left.

Once your packages are opened you might want to consider transferring the contents to airtight containers to keep out humidity and bugs. If you are plagued with bugs, you can put some items in the refrigerator or freezer without causing damage to them.

I keep all my rice and pasta in the freezer because I don't use them every day. When I lived in Florida, I put all my cereals in airtight containers because of the high humidity. It really depends on where you live. In Arizona, I used the cereal out of the box because there was no humidity to worry about and the cereal was used daily. However, boll weevils were a problem with flour and rice, so those were kept in airtight containers.

Put canned goods all together on another shelf, again grouping like items, such as all your soups together in one area — all fruits together in one area — all vegetables together in one area — all sauces together in one area, etc..

If you want to get **Really** organized, you can be brave and alphabetize the cans in each group, such as: Beans, Corn, Peas, Zucchini in your vegetable section! (I personally wouldn't attempt to alphabetize within these groups ((like lima beans, navy beans and pinto beans all lined up in a row)), unless you have a secret desire for punishment!)

For those with perfection tendencies, or if you have OCD, I would avoid this altogether. Save your perfection for bigger challenges that are worth the effort.

Grouping all of these like items together makes it easier for you to find what you're looking for, as well as making it easier for you to make a shopping list. It's obvious that you don't need to buy tomato sauce when you already have ten cans on the shelf that you can clearly see.

The reason I have gone somewhat into detail on grouping the canned items is because of my client, Herb.

Herb

Herb's comment to me when we started working was, "I always seem to run out of soup, but I always seem to be buying soup!' We opened his kitchen cupboards and started grouping all the canned items. He was aghast to discover that he had 20 cans of soup! Poor thing, I thought he'd have a heart attack. He and his roommates were in the habit of opening a cabinet and just placing items into any convenient "hole" that they saw. What did they know! No one ever explained grouping to them or showed them how to handle their groceries. Herb's much happier now and so are his roommates — he's quit screaming at them for stealing his soup!

When you buy in large quantities, you need space for all the cans, plus it's helpful if you can see them instead of going by memory. (When I talk about buying in large quantity, I am not referring to the year's storage that the Mormons practice. That's another 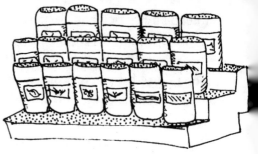 visit!) Let's look at your shelving and some options available when you buy in bulk:

- "Expand-A-Shelf," found in kitchen stores (like Lechters), linen stores (like Linens 'N Things), and variety stores (like Target, K-mart, Wal-Mart), work great in cupboards to help you see items on the back of shelves, especially in pantries. These plastic shelves look like three steps. They come in different "step" sizes to accommodate small containers (like prescriptions), medium containers (like spices), and larger containers (like canned goods). With these shelf inserts there's no more moving everything out of the way to find what's hiding in back.

Some shelves in pantries are quite high, so the Expand-A-Shelf may not be the best buy. You might try adding a half-shelf at the back of the pantry. Or buy the vinyl coated wire shelving units that are now available.

- If your pantry shelf has enough room, you could possibly stack two of these wire shelves on top of each other. Be sure to stack only like items together so you don't go through another digging process.

Sometimes you can use a combination of the two different shelves, with the shelf to the back for large tall items, and the Expand-A-Shelf in the front. You have to be careful, however, that the items on the top shelf of the Expand-A-Shelf don't fall off the back!

- Then there are turntables, which are also excellent for high, remote areas of cupboards. When you do use turntables on high shelves, keep the products to the outer edge of the turntable. Hiding things behind the front product will defeat the purpose of quick finding. Don't forget an easily accessible step stool to get at those top shelves.

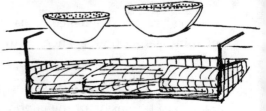

- An option for very tall shelves is a small three-sided vinyl coated wire basket that hooks to the shelf above by brackets and hangs beneath that shelf into the lower shelf. This is good for some smaller items that you might want to have right at your fingertips, rather than digging around for them. This item can also be found at kitchen stores, among others.

Some upper cupboards are very deep and everyone tends to stash things in them that they seldom use. These cupboards can usually be found above the refrigerator, above the stove, and above the wall type pantry unit. The wall pantry unit's upper cupboard contains way too many items that, once in, are never seen again. An option for these problem areas is:

- Install roll out shelves so this area can be more accessible to you. You can still put items up there that you seldom use, but at least you'll be able to see what you want to get down and you might be able to do so without the use of a stepladder.

- Other items that we have to deal with are all those plastic bowls that we collect. I know that all of us keep used bowls – from butter and Cool-Whip bowls to yogurt bowls. For leftovers, right? And I also know that we collect Rubbermaid bowls and Tupperware bowls. For leftovers, of course! But, my client Inga just plain liked them!

Inga

Inga had every combination of Tupperware that you could possibly imagine. She had just moved into a new house and there just wasn't any room for all of it, let alone any of her regular kitchen items. In addition to the newer Tupperware items, Inga also had all of the older ones. You know – the orange, brown and avocado green ones. She knew she had too many. It was really hard for her, but she finally decided to box up the older sets and put them in the garage. She agreed that if she didn't use them by the same time next year that she would donate them to a half-way house for abused kids. She would also work on seeing how many of the items she was keeping that she actually used all the time. The items that were not used would also be boxed up for storage in the garage. Inga is a little compulsive about buying things, so she had to agree to not buy any more Tupperware or any other containers, no matter what.

If you have an abundance of plastic bowls and lids, try setting smaller bowls into larger bowls. Then set the batch of bowls on top of all the lids.

You can also put bowls on top of the largest lids, with the smaller lids corralled in a container that sits next to the bowls or, buy a lid holder and attach it to the inside of the cupboard door.

I personally prefer to keep the lids on the individual bowls so that I know each bowl has a lid, and that I can find it when I want it. I have to admit that I go a little crazy when I can't find the lid! I throw out any bowl without a lid (or you have **Clutter Start!**).

My daughter gives these topless bowls to her gardening husband for use as a planter until the plant is ready to go outdoors.

Again, if your cupboards have a lot of height and you're storing the plastic bowls there, you might want to think about putting in another full shelf, or buying the wire shelving units so that you can stack these plastic containers easier.

Don't neglect the outside surfaces of upper cabinets either.

- You can keep placemats handy by putting them on a very large clip that hangs inside or outside of a cupboard,

- or on the side of the refrigerator on a magnetic clip holder. Everyone I know puts placemats in a kitchen drawer, taking up space needed for other things.

- You can also hang some utensils from cupboard doors, as well as pot holders and dish towels. Be careful how much you hang on the out side, however, or you'll get that cluttery look again.

Wall Storage

Walls are a much ignored area. When you have limited cupboard space, start by taking a look at your walls.

- You can attach pegboards to the walls to hold pots and pans, or hang the white vinyl coated wire units that hug the walls. Hooks hold whatever items you want to hang.

- You can also hang the wire units from the ceiling and hang pots and pans, baskets, utensils, etc. from them. Watch out, Martha Stewart! We may even come up with items she's not thought of!

If you hang items from your ceiling or wall be sure that you have enough clearance to safely walk beneath.

- The pegboards, which are made of a thick cardboard material or fiberboard, would probably be less expensive than the wire racks. And you could paint them so that they would blend with your wall color. Or paint some wild design on it! Have fun!

Some people really have an aversion to anything on their walls, so if this is the case, then I would suggest investing in a portable pantry, like the ones that Rubbermaid sells. The shelves can be easily moved and it's strong enough to hold heavy items. It certainly isn't pretty, but when storage space is needed, it does the trick. If you're at all creative, maybe some artwork on the doors would spark it up a bit.

Cupboards, Lower

Let's take a look at how we can find storage in our lower cupboard areas.

Undersink Storage

- Cleaning products in the kitchen are probably under the kitchen sink. You can install roll out containers for these items so that they are corralled and easy to get to.

- You can also use long cardboard boxes that you can pull out. These don't pull out as easily as the roll out unit, but they definitely cost less!

- If you have crawling children in the house, I recommend putting child-safe locks on the cupboard doors. When they start to walk and get really curious it's best to remove all these products from beneath the sink and look elsewhere for storage.

- When you don't have surplus cleaning products, put them in the cupboard over the stove on a small turntable. This generally is a cupboard that has no other useful purpose, except possibly for items you rarely use. This might be the place to put your cleaning products when your children start crawling/walking. But, be aware of flammable items and store them elsewhere.

- Under the sink also seems to be the favorite place for garbage cans. If you do want your trash can(s) beneath the sink, get one that is easy to put things into. If you get one with a lid you're asking for total frustration.

- If you like to recycle items, buy smaller trash cans that can also fit beneath the sink. When you put a plastic grocery bag in these smaller containers, you are recycling even more.

- If you have no room under the sink for trash cans, then you'll need to have a can with a lid on it. Look for one that you can open by stepping on a peddle so you don't have to fumble with the lid. For recycling, The Container Store, among others, sell a recycling center that fits in some kitchens. It doesn't take up a lot of space and is made of a sturdy plastic with three side-by-side holding areas.

SPECIAL NEEDS
If you have use of your upper body but are in a wheelchair, your kitchen set-up will need to be customized for your needs.

Generally it will be best for you to have your dishes in the lower cupboards. There are roll-out shelves available which attach to the bottom of cabinets and hold up to 100 lbs.

Your pots and pans will also need to be at this level for you.

For the lighter items, you can keep them in the upper cupboards and we using a grabbing mechanism at the end of a pole to retrieve the items.

If you're having your kitchen built to be more accessible for you, be sure you leave enough clearance for your wheelchair when the lower cupboard doors are open and the shelves are pulled out.

If your space is really limited, you might consider leaving the cupboard doors off so that the retrieval of items is a little easier for you.

POINTS TO PONDER

Many people like to keep the kitchen towels, cloths and potholders in a kitchen drawer. Sometimes, there just isn't enough room for that luxury. If you have a pantry with very tall shelves, you can use a wire under-shelf holder for these items, or the pantry shelf itself. If you don't store anything above the refrigerator that you need to get to often, buy a nice container for the top of the refrigerator and put the towels and cloths in it. You can put the potholders in it also, and keep one near the stove on a hook. But not too near the stove! We don't want any fires! If you have enough counter space, you could even buy a nice container or basket for the counter and put the towels there. Also, see "drawer" section below.

For those with learning disabilities (Attention Deficit Disorder, dyslexia, etc.) I would highly recommend labeling all your cupboards on the outside and inside. If you use clear tape on the cupboards it will look nicer than white tape and not be so obvious.

You can have a general category listing on the outside that says "dishes," and on the inside, label each shelf: "plates," "bowls," "glasses," etc. This will keep you from putting things in different places and will also help others who may be helping you in the kitchen.

Jenna

Jenna is dyslexic and was quite frustrated when she couldn't find what she was looking for. She, of course, knew that her dishes were in the cupboard but invariably went to the wrong one. It also destroyed her morale when relatives would visit and then help with the dishes. They would put things away for her and then she really had no idea where to find a particular dish she wanted. When she labeled her cupboards both she and her relatives were delighted. No one had to distract her to ask where something was, or where it belonged. Also, be sure to read the following "hoarding" information.

For all of you with "hoarding issues," I offer the following suggestions:

- Remove all the dishes from your kitchen cupboards and place them on your counters. Pick out enough dishes for each person in the family for three (3) meals. In other words, for one person, have three plates, three glasses, three cups, etc., for everyone. If there are two of you, then you'll have six plates, etc. This will give you enough dishes to eat on and not require you to immediately wash the dirty ones.

- Get a sturdy plastic storage container with a tight fitting lid on it. Take all the extra dishes, carefully wrap them in bubble wrap or lots of white tissue paper. If you must use newspaper, wrap your dishes in a plastic bag first so that the newsprint doesn't rub off onto your dishes. Put the dishes into the plastic container. Label the container, and date it. Store this container in the garage, in the attic, under the stairwell, outside of the house in an area that you don't use, or in an outdoor storage unit.

- **Do Not** invest in a storage facility that you have to pay money for. This invites more items to be stored and feeds into your hoarding problem.

- You can also store your china this way if you have no room for it. Most of us only use our china during holidays, so if you carefully wrap your china, all you'll need to do is bring the container in the house and unpack it. Your dishes will still be clean, while most china cabinets still let dust filter in.

- If you have company, you'll likely have enough dishes on your shelves, if you've kept the dishes washed. But if you need more, retrieve some dishes from the stored container.

- If you find that you really don't use the extra dishes that you've stored, think about giving them to someone who can really use them.

Many of my "hoarding" clients are happier giving their items to people who really need them rather than selling them or giving them away to the "stuff collecting" truck. I know that you don't want just anyone having your things, so check with your particular place of worship, or even the Red Cross, as to who could benefit by your donation.

Drawers

Homework: buy two utensil holders (yes, I'm giving you permission to buy – but read this first).

- In one, put all your knives, forks and spoons.

- In the other put your long wooden or metal spoons and spatulas.

- Corn picks and ice cream scoops can share this holder, as well as all those annoying little things that are on your counter tops or floating free in a drawer somewhere.

If you live in an apartment, or an older home, some of the drawers are too narrow for the utensil holders. Not to fear! Almost all grocery stores and variety stores carry single utensil holders, which are generally white plastic and "hook" to each other. You can create your own holders with these single units.

If you keep kitchen towels in a drawer rather than the linen closet, keep them in the lower drawers so that the upper drawers carry the items you use on a daily or frequent basis.

You can fold your towels so they fit in your drawers vertically (on their edges), rather than stacking them. They'll be easier to retrieve and you can get more in the drawer.

INSTRUCTIONS FOR FOLDING THE TOWELS

Fold the towel in three sections, lengthwise. Then fold it in half by taking one end to meet the other end. Does it stand in the drawer, or is it too tall? If it's too tall, fold it in half again. If this makes it too bulky, unfold it until you're back at the three sections. Now, from top to bottom, fold the towel in thirds. This should now fit the drawer without being too bulky. Each drawer is going to be different, so you'll have to experiment with the folding.

• If you don't want to fold at all, and would just like to throw the towels into the drawer, then do so. Just be sure that all you have in that drawer are the towels and nothing else.

• You can fold the washcloths the same way and also stack them upright. If you have room, you can put them in the same drawer with the towels.

Do you throw your pot holders in any open convenient drawer? Try these options:

- Underneath the upper cupboard that is nearest your stove, screw in cup hooks and hang your potholders that you use all the time.

- Hang your pot holders from magnetic hooks that you can put on your stove or refrigerator. (This will only work if your stove and refrigerator are metal and not plastic.)

WARNING
Be sure that the pot holder is away from any possible heat source from the stove. That was my own personal lesson after burning up my cupboard and ceiling. We won't even talk about what my husband and landlord had to say! Of course, that was when I was VERY young!

Junk Drawer

It's best to have just one junk drawer. Some of my organizing associates disagree with this totally, but I give you permission to have ONE. We ADD people need it!

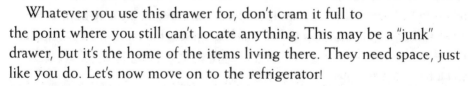

- Corral as much as you can with small plastic bins.
- Ice cube trays work well for needles, nails, push-pins, coins, etc.
- This drawer can hold matches, keys, scissors, note pads, pencils, etc.
- It can also hold extra telephone cords or electrical cords bound inside toilet paper rolls, or rubber bands.

Whatever you use this drawer for, don't cram it full to the point where you still can't locate anything. This may be a "junk" drawer, but it's the home of the items living there. They need space, just like you do. Let's now move on to the refrigerator!

Refrigerator

Speaking of junk drawers, guess what your refrigerator is? The biggest junk drawer of all!

Let's see what "junk" we put into this drawer:

We eat out and put our leftovers in this massive unit – then we buy fresh fruits and vegetables and shove them into the crisper bins, never to be seen again. Then we go shopping again and throw out what we've put in the refrigerator the month before!

We buy frozen foods and pile it in the freezer in front of, or on top of earlier frozen foods – and then try to unearth something that we bought six months ago.

We do this month after month. How do we handle all this stuff when we've got all the other stuff to handle? Breathe! Here are some ideas:

- One way to avoid the odors of old food is to throw it out before your shopping trip and wipe down the shelves so that when groceries are put away they aren't picking up the odors from the old food.

- If you must keep leftovers (even those from restaurants), put them in clear plastic containers, label what it is and the date you put it in the refrigerator.

- Keep all your leftovers on one shelf in the refrigerator so you know exactly where to go for them when you want them. The top shelf works well as it's usually where we put our milk, juice and butter. Every time you go for milk or juice, you'll see the leftovers.

- Check the dates on leftovers daily and throw out anything older than a few days. The smell after one week is definitely not pleasant! Plus, the FDA says that leftovers should be used within 72 hours. That's only three days! Excuse me, I need to go check something ...it's OK, I have another day left!

- Try to keep all condiment items together so you can grab them quickly when you want them. The jars or bottles that condiments come in should be dated.

- If you don't use olives very often, buy the smaller cans or jars. If you have an open jar, you might not want to eat them if they're really old.

- Remember, when you open mayonnaise, ketchup, bar-b-que sauce, mustard, etc., it needs to be put in the refrigerator.

- Fruits and vegetables should be cleaned and thoroughly dried before putting them into the crisper bins. Putting them into ventilated plastic vegetable bags keeps them fresher for a longer period of time.

- If you use vegetables in salads, or for stir-frys, it would be easier on you if you clean and chop up the vegetables all at one time. Get the family together and make this a project. You can then bag the different vegetables, thereby making them easier to use at dinner time. As usual, label and date the bags.

All of the labeling and dating is doubly important in the freezer.

- If you have a chest freezer, it's critical to label, date and rotate the packages of food.

- Always rotate the older foods to the top when putting in newer foods. Specially designed baskets are available for chest freezers to make this process easier.

- If you can't find the baskets, use plastic stacking bins.

- Depending on the types of food you're storing, try to categorize them. Keep all beef, chicken, turkey, etc., in different areas. For instance, put all "meat" items to the left and all "fowl" items to the right. Or put them in different baskets. Do the same with frozen vegetables, breakfast items, ice cream, etc.

- Keep an inventory list attached to the inside or outside of the freezer so that you know what is lurking inside, and where.

- When you use the last package or two of something you eat frequently, add it to your shopping list. Teach your family to write down items also. It's pretty hard for you to always go into the refrigerator or freezer to see what's left and what needs to be bought.

Upright and side-by-side refridgerator/freezers need the same care as the chest freezer.

- Packages must be labeled, dated, inventoried and rotated.

- Use the different shelves to separate your different meat items, etc. The side-by-side refridgerator/freezer gives you much less room than the chest and upright models, but it's perfect for a small family or for those who don't rely too much on frozen foods.

- I have a side-by-side refrigerator freezer and I store all my pastas, rice and bread in it. I also store extra packages of flour and sugar in the freezer. A home economist may be screaming right now, but at least I don't have to contend with bugs when I want to use those items.

Advantages of Having a Refrigerator

Another thing that these giant junk drawers offer is a place to display our loved one's (children's) art work!

- Keep art objects on the refrigerator for just one week then transfer the best one (with the child's help) to a 3-ring binder;
- or put the best in a frame;
- or put the best on a large corkboard,
- or put the best in a memory box with the child's name on it.
- After one month you again pick out the best one.
- After three months, you again pick out the best one. The idea is to help them make choices, in addition to avoiding "hoarding" problems. See more on this in the Children's chapter.

Besides art work, the refrigerator is also a handy place for your shopping inventory:

- Put a small magnetic container, approximately 5" x 7", on the front of the 'fridge and keep a writing tablet and pencil in it for a grocery list.
- You can keep store and manufacturer's coupons in an envelope behind the tablet, or in a specially designed "wallet" that stores them by expiration date and/or type of item.
- When you list an item on your grocery list that you have a coupon for, pull the coupon out of the envelope and leave it in the container. When you go shopping, just grab your list and coupons!
- When you know which recipes you want to cook for the week (or month, depending on how often you shop), put those recipe index cards (see Cooking section below) in the container with your grocery list also.

Cooking – Some Time Saving Ideas

Gaining some sanity and stress relief at mealtime is a much sought after commodity. Stress creates enough "mind clutter" without adding mealtime clutter to the equation.

When our households are clutter free and we can find what we are looking for, life seems just a little easier.

Since we have attacked several rooms of the house and learned how to get rid of clutter, let's slow down a bit and see how we can make meals a little simpler.

- At mealtime, occasionally use bagged salads instead of making a salad from scratch. They include all the ingredients and you can still add your own touches. Add chicken, shrimp, or meat to some of the salads and you have a nice main dish. Yes, it costs more than making it from scratch, but the pennies are worth it when you're tired and rushed.

- Other bagged items that you can buy are shrimp, cheese, vegetables, and cut-up fruits.

- Some specialty stores, as well as grocery stores, also carry ready-made sandwiches, salads and complete meals. You can even buy a complete turkey dinner – cooked! **Can You Imagine** really eating with the family on Thanksgiving rather than spending it in the kitchen?

- Keep 30 favorite recipes on separate index cards listing all needed ingredients. Use a new card each day you need to cook. When you've made the meal, move the card to the back. You'll have enough recipes to keep meals from getting boring. No more, "Oh, it's Tuesday so it must be pot roast!" remarks. Rotate these cards in a card box of some type so that you are not making the same meals all the time. Pull out the cards you will be using for the week and put them with your grocery list so you don't forget any of the ingredients. This also eliminates having to write the items again on the list. Now you're all ready to shop with your list, your recipes and your coupons!

KITCHEN CHATTER

- **Buy a space-saver water container with a spigot. They are just a few inches wide and fit vertically in the refrigerator, from front to back. No more common bottle that everyone drinks out of. The containers can be found at The Container Store and some variety stores.**
- **Refrigerated candles tend to burn longer and are easily accessible in case of emergency. Keep them in a container, rather than loose on the shelf.**
- **When you open the last item of something (like toothpaste), or when 3 items are left of something you use often (like toilet paper), put it on the grocery list.**

- An ammonia and water solution is a quick, effective and inexpensive cleaner that will not streak. It works for all windows, ceramic or tile floors (NOT WOOD), counters and all appliances. Use one part ammonia to two parts water.
- For the religious groups that store foods for up to a year, buy roll-out shelves that allow you to rotate your cans and packaged goods easily. Put new cans to the rear of the shelf and use the ones in front. If you're going to store your canned goods in the garage, be sure to put them in a contained storage unit that will help keep out the moisture and dirt.

It's time to get the kids involved

- Show the kids how to cook their favorite meals and let them decide what night they want to cook. Parental discretion is needed here as one eight-year-old might be capable, but another may not. You may have to help them with a portion of the meal but it will give them some pride, and future independence.
- Have them put their favorite recipes on index cards also.
- Then when ALL of you go shopping you can teach them how to buy the ingredients they are going to need.

The following suggestion is offered to those who enjoy their family around while cooking meals. If this "mob" in the kitchen vicinity causes you to pull your hair out, please ignore it, groan through it, or laugh through it. You won't hurt my feelings, I'm only offering it as a suggestion.

Sometimes people with ADD can handle many people around them, while others can not. And sometimes people without ADD go "nuts" when anyone is in the kitchen, including the dog!

And this suggestion doesn't mean that you have to do it every night! The kids might enjoy having a "special" day.

My suggestion: have a "gab fest" while you cook

- Let the children tell you what has transpired in their day at school. It's a good time to talk about any questions they have about life, love or school.

- Have craft projects ready, or games, etc., that younger kids can do on their own at the kitchen table.

- Put the baby in the high chair (away from the stove), or in a chair carrier that you can put on the counter while you cook. This allows you to get dinner done while keeping an eye on everyone.

- Older children can do their homework, help with dinner, or do chores.

- If the older children are doing homework and need some quiet, try telling the younger kids that they, too, need to do their homework (coloring or reading) and must be quiet so everyone can concentrate. It makes them feel grown up. I'm big on having the whole family involved together at this time. It's probably the only time that some families have together, and it creates some wonderful memories.

- Avoid answering your telephone at this time. If you work outside the home, your children need some extra attention. If you work at home, it may be the only real family time you all have together.

- When dinner is almost ready have everyone set the table, dividing chores according to age and height. Why height? It's pretty tough for a three year old to reach dishes in an upper cabinet without your stopping what you're doing to help them. The whole idea is to give you some aid, not create more work for yourself.

- After dinner they can clear the table and rinse dishes – maybe even put them into the dishwasher. If you do not have a dishwasher then show them how to wash their own plates, bowls and silverware. This means that they have to take turns at the sink, but it also means that they will continue on toward adulthood knowing how to fend for themselves.

Summary

- When your kitchen and home is in order, life is less stressful because your peace at home carries through all areas of your life.

- Counters can be cleared of infrequently used items by placing in lower cupboards or elsewhere.

- Upper cupboards are where we can stack plates, bowls, glasses, cups and saucers, packaged goods and canned items.

- When stacking plates, etc., keep them all together, rather than putting some plates on one shelf and some on another.

- Walls are also available for storage of utensils, pots and pans, pot holders, etc.

- Lower cupboards are where we can store pots and pans and items that we don't use too often. Because these items are heavy, pull-out shelves can be used.

- Drawers are useful for eating utensils, kitchen towels, pot holders and organized "junk."
- The refrigerator is useful for art work, holding shopping lists, attaching placemats to and storing food!
- The whole family can be involved in cooking and shopping.
- Keep 30 days worth of recipes so meals are never boring.
- Have a gab fest with your children while cooking dinner.

Now, I Will:

- clear my counters! (I need my can opener every day, my toaster, my coffee maker and my microwave.) Everything else goes!
- store the extra dishes that I want, but the rest is going to the half-way house – or shelter – or to someone I know that is in need.

I Will:

- use every bit of wall storage space that I can without making things look cluttery.
- not fill up every open space or cupboard and will strive to not collect stuff.
- use my refrigerator and freezer wisely by dating everything that goes into it – and on it!
- encourage my family members to be together during meal times and to help with cleanup, cooking and shopping – YES, you can!

Look at your kitchen now. Clear, shiny counters. Your coffee or tea pot ready and waiting with your favorite brew. And the can opener and toaster oven just sitting there smiling at you because all those other pesky appliances aren't bothering them! It's time to start inviting guests in – go on! You've cleared the cobwebs at the front door and have cleared the foyer, living room, dining room, family room and kitchen. They don't need to see your bedrooms! Oh, oh, what if they have to go to the bathroom – we better tackle that one next!

Ready for that trip down the hall to the bathroom? Yes, you are! Smile, look at all you've done so far. Pat yourself on the back! Grab that garbage can and let's go – don't forget to eat first and take your meds, if necessary.

CHAPTER SIX

Busy Little Room

A Look at Your Bathroom

Bathrooms are sometimes small rooms, however, much business takes place in them and we certainly use lots of equipment in them. Nothing worse than a messy bathroom unless it's a cluttered kitchen counter. Necessary work is hard to do in either place when it's messy.

Just like the kitchen, the bathroom also causes fits for many people. Especially if it's a small room where many people want to put "lots of stuff." What kind of stuff do all of us want to squirrel away? Well, if you're a man, you'll store soaps, deodorants, brushes, combs, shaving creams, lotions, aftershaves, razors (manual and electric), all the toothbrushes, toothpaste and dental floss that dentists give away, mouthwashes, papers pulled out of pockets, movie stubs, etc.

If you're a woman, you'll store perfume, lotions, soaps, deodorants, curling iron, hair dryer, all the toothbrushes, toothpaste and dental floss that dentists give away, mouthwashes, coupons, brushes, combs and makeup.

Some of you may even have first aid items in your bathrooms, if it can fit in with all the other stuff.

If children are sharing these bathrooms, then we have to include all their stuff – toothbrushes, toys, etc.

TIP
Keep a fingertip towel available and wipe up water splashes from the sink top and mirror after each use. It keeps the bathroom looking cleaner even if you haven't cleaned it! Also keep a squeegee in the shower.

So, how do you exist in a bathroom that's shared, or even one that you have all to yourself and all your stuff?

You exist by carefully containerizing what you have. Containers in themselves set limits and help us to really see what we're keeping. Just remember, though, that the containers themselves need to be stored, so don't think that you can containerize the world and have it fit into this tiny place!

What are potential storage areas where we can containerize? Here are some ideas:

- under sinks, in storage bins;
- over the toilet, on shelving units;
- on the toilet tank top, in baskets;
- on countertops, in special containers;
- inside drawers, in small containers;
- on window sills, in small containers;
- with wall units, in varying heights and widths;
- on the floor, in decorative containers;
- and in the medicine cabinet.

Let's explore some of these options.

Under Sinks

- Before buying containers for under the sink, measure the area under and around plumbing so you buy things that will fit in the space.

- Use bins that can be easily pulled out to corral items. These bins can be plastic, or cardboard. Some plastic bins have runners on the bottom that you attach with screws to the bottom of the vanity so they are easy to pull out. As in the kitchen, you can have pull-out bins built in.

- Cardboard boxes can also be used in this area. Depending on the room you have, you may have to cut down the sides of the box a bit in order for it to fit beneath the sink. Boxes work just as well as the plastic containers and are obviously less expensive.

- Another option is to buy the two-or four-drawer plastic containers that Rubbermaid and other companies make.

- The drawer containers work especially well when you do not have a vanity beneath your sink.

- You can put skirting around the sink to hide what's beneath; however, skirting usually doesn't appeal to men, so be careful in your choice of pattern.

- Some drawer containers have see-through fronts, but the ones you cannot see through may be more appealing to those of you who don't want to see what you've jammed in the drawers.

- Some people with Attention Deficit Disorders might find the see-through drawers more useful so that you don't have to guess what's inside.

- Many people with ADD and dyslexia find that labeling the drawers is also very useful so that there is no guesswork about where to return something, or where it is when you need to find it. Like we did in the kitchen, you can label the drawers with clear tape and black ink, or find pictures to paste on.

- This type of vanity or under-sink storage is also useful for people in wheelchairs. The drawers fit against the wall, giving enough room to get close to the sink when there is no sink vanity. You can also roll up your extra towels and put them in these drawers.

- In addition to all the toiletries that can be stored in these drawers, under most sinks you will find that two packages of toilet paper (4 rolls each) fit nicely on top of the drawers laying down, side by side. No more running out to the hall closet or elsewhere to get toilet paper.

- Or, you can store the toilet paper in the drawers. It depends on the size of the drawers.

- If you don't like the idea of drawers, or pull out bins, try some baskets, large, small, or mixed. They are certainly lightweight, and you can just grab the handle and pull it out. This, of course, depends on what you'll put in it. Heavy items may make using baskets a little impractical. On the other hand, it might also keep the clutter down as you can get just so much stuff into a basket. Options!

- Since it's easier to have cleaning supplies where you use them, keep a small supply beneath the sink in one of these containers. However, if you have small children in the house then you'll still need to look for higher areas to store these items.

- For compulsive hoarders – I recommend that only two of these drawer containers be used. You can fill the drawers, but once they're full, that's it. Avoid, at all cost, buying another unit.

- The only way to stop the hoarding is to allow yourself a limited space to keep necessary items and to avoid adding anything to that space.

- Necessary items means that you limit every product you use to just one item. So if you use mascara, you may have one tube – not one tube of different manufacturers. If you use different colored mascara, still limit yourself to one of each.

- Try to limit also the number of lipsticks that you keep. If you have many, see which ones you use all the time and put the others away some place. See if you really look to use a lipstick that you've put away.

- Three to five lipsticks should be a limit that you strive for. I know this will be hard for some of you, but please try. You did say that you were ready, didn't you? Smile, wipe your tears and let's go on. I'm not trying to punish you, I really am trying to help.

Let's go on and take a look at the drawers in the vanity itself.

Vanity Drawers

- For the drawers that are in the vanity itself, use small plastic bins to corral makeup and other small toiletries.

- Again, if you don't want to spend money, you can use small cardboard boxes, old dishes, checkbook boxes or anything else that will fit in the drawer and has enough of a "lip" on it to keep items inside while moving the drawer in and out. Tape the underside of the boxes to the floor of drawer so they don't shift when opening and shutting the drawer.

The whole idea is to keep like items together so that when you reach for a lipstick, or an aftershave, you know exactly where it is.

As it is written,

"be not righteous over much..." (Ecclesiastes 7:16.).

In order to do this when we share a bathroom, we need some more options.

- If you are sharing the vanity, assign "sides." Have soap dishes for each side, as well as cups, if necessary. Throw-away Dixie cups in a dispenser are really better. You avoid germs and cleanup.

- If you have to share a drawer, the only sane way to do it is to have a container for each person's belongings.

- If you have to deal with a hair dryer and curling iron, buy a holder that can be installed on the inside of the vanity door or on the wall if there is no vanity.

And let's not forget the "medicine" cabinet.

Medicine Cabinet

If your bathroom is shared by many people and has only one medicine cabinet, consider getting an upright clear plastic kitchen silverware holder that sits on a counter. Several toothbrushes can be put into this container, along with toothpaste, cotton swabs, Q-tips, etc. The plastic allows it to get wet without getting ruined.

Try to look at containers of all sorts for different ways of storing items, anywhere in your home. Although it doesn't have anything to do with the bathroom, one of my clients found a "different" storage area:

- As for the medicine cabinet, put items in it that are used every day but aren't really handy in a drawer. Your toothbrush, toothpaste and deodorant are an example.

- Larger items (hairspray, face washes, handcreams, etc.) are also better in the medicine cabinet. Again, if you're sharing this space, assign shelves.

Kim

Kim had just moved into a home and because of her Attention Deficit Hyperactivity Disorder (ADHD) had some household help to clean and take care of her children while she ran her business. At night she was forever looking for the diapers and would find them in different places, most anywhere in her two-story house. On one of her buying trips to India she brought back some decorative open weave "suitcases." After we started working together she caught on to the idea of containerizing and having a home for everything. Her solution to the diaper problem was to use one of the suitcases as a storage place for the diapers, wipes and creams. Her household help knew exactly where to put the diapers and Kim no longer had to be frustrated looking for the diapers.

"A cheerful heart is good medicine..." (Proverbs 17:22.)

TOOTHPASTE CHATTER

Have the kids get rid of their toothpaste mess with toilet paper or paper toweling that you keep beneath the sink. Let your children know that the paper toweling should be put in the waste can, not the toilet.

- Storing medicines in bathrooms isn't too great an idea, however. Sometimes temperature and humidity are bad for certain prescriptions.

- If you have small children in the home, the medicine cabinet is **Definitely Not** the place to put medicine, even on a top shelf.

- The same applies to perfumes and lotions when you have little children. I learned this the hard way **Many** years ago.

My tale

My 18-month-old and two-year-old daughters decided to climb on the toilet and then onto the vanity. (I was safely out of sight taking care of the laundry.)

After opening the medicine cabinet they took out my husband's aftershave and drank it! Imagine this: You have no car and don't know anyone where you live because you just moved in. Your children are in trouble. You call the hospital and they tell you to bring them in now. No, they can't send an ambulance (you have no insurance). You can't afford a taxicab. What to do?

I called the police to see if they could at least get me to the hospital. Yes, they could. When they showed up, it was in a "paddy wagon." I was mortified! And my neighbors were peering out their windows like I was a major gangster! (This WAS Chicago, after all.)

Believe me, you don't want to go to the emergency room in this manner to watch your children having their stomachs pumped thinking what a terrible mother you are! And of course, all those questions from your "concerned" neighbors!

If you have small children in the house, don't forget to install safety locks on all cabinets and drawers. Bathrooms are notoriously loaded with harmful substances.

And another word of caution for those of you with hoarding issues: Just because you may live alone doesn't mean that you MUST fill up every space available.

Limit yourself so that you're not tempted to keep putting away more stuff, e.g., not ten combs, old toothbrushes, dried mascara tubes, etc. (In with the new, out with the old.)

You also might want to reconsider putting any breakable items in this cabinet. Anyone in earthquake country knows what a disaster that can cause.

So with all the restrictions on medicine cabinets, what can you use this space for? As stated above:

- toothpaste,
- toothbrushes,
- deodorant,
- cotton balls,
- Q-tips,
- combs,
- brushes,
- emery boards and anything else that can't be drunk or chewed and swallowed.

Depending on the age and curiosity of your child(ren) you might want to re-think the cotton balls, Q-tips and deodorant! They can be eaten or put into ears and noses.

As long as you have children in the house, the medicine cabinet should remain as child safe as possible. Medicines can be put in a high kitchen cupboard away from the stove, in a dresser drawer or any other spot that you feel is safe from any child, any age.

What do you do with the dirty clothes you leave in the bathroom? Well, forget it, the floor is **not** an option!

Dirty Clothes

Many people use hampers for dirty clothing. If you prefer one in your bathroom, buy a size that will fit in the room without hindering movement to the toilet or the bathtub/shower.

- Hampers come in different shapes: round, oblong, square and some that even fit into corners or hang over the door (made of netting).

- If you really hate hampers, but want the dirty clothes in the bath room, then use the space beneath the vanity. This means, of course, that you have lost that storage space for other items.

- The other option would be to hang a laundry bag from a hook on the back of the door. If you have company sharing that bathroom this particular idea isn't going to win you a gold star from them as the door probably keeps closing on them because the bag is so full!

Another storage area that is widely used, but seldom thought about, is the window.

Windows

Some homes and apartment bathrooms have windows, with a ledge large enough to hold large bottles. Some items to use in this space are:

- shampoo bottles;

- razors (if this ledge is high enough and children can not reach it, it does provide a good storage area);

- oils and specialty lotions;

- a decorative plastic or wicker container with silk flowers can also be placed on this window ledge as long as it's the proper size. Adhere the bottom of the container to the window ledge.

Some people may need to put curtains on their bathroom windows. Instead of drilling holes and putting up curtain rods, buy a strong tension rod and hang the curtains from it by placing the rod inside the window framing, if there's room. You can find these rods at most variety stores.

There are also other storage options that we can use in this bathroom. Let's take a look.

Non-standard Bathroom Storage Options

Some people like to keep towels in the bathroom rather than in a linen closet. For many, however, this creates a big problem since there is little room. Therefore:

- roll up towels and washcloths and place them in a pretty basket. The basket can be put on the floor, or on a vanity chair, or on the tub ledge;

- purchase shelving that fits against the wall, over the toilet tank, preferably made of plastic or wicker because of the moisture in this room. Some of these units come with a shelf that has doors on it where you can put some toiletry items or toilet paper;

- buy a fairly new item called a "spacesaver" by Rubbermaid and other companies. It fits between the vanity and the toilet. You can't store much in it, but it will hold toilet paper and some towels;

- if your bathroom is spacious enough, but lacking a vanity or linen closet, you can buy some shelving units or an etagere that is made of wicker that fit into bathrooms nicely and seem to hold up to the humidity.

New York Organizer, Peggy Peckham of In-House Organizers, suggests using real shelves, specifically, bookcases. Can't you just see it? (Well ...I do!) A small two or three-shelf white wicker bookcase hanging from the wall holding all your different colored rolled up towels? What a stunning decorative touch, especially if it's across from a mirror.

What about the ordinary things in the bathroom, like towels? Funny you should ask!

- For the day-to-day storage of each individual's personal towel, sturdy hooks are a great addition. This is especially true for children, and can be in addition to or in place of towel racks.

- Curtain hooks that hang over the curtain rods are also good to hang towels from, on the inside towards the shower or tub. Hint: Assign everyone different colored towels. When a towel winds up on the floor, you'll know whose ear to grab.

- If you can't afford to buy different colors, sew on name labels, or use an indelible marker and mark the label with numbers. Number 1 is you or your spouse, the first born is number 2 or 3, and so on. Guests get unmarked towels.

- There have been many articles written about color coding. Some suggest matching everything used (toothbrush, comb, etc.) to one specific child. Since kids get bored easily, I'm not sure if color coding everything is the answer. However, if you think that it'll work, go for it.

...and what about toilet paper ...and kids bathtub toys ...and...

- If you don't want people rummaging around in your vanity for toilet paper, or elsewhere, there are other ways to store the toilet paper. Take a toilet plunger, paint the handle to match your bathroom colors and put the toilet paper on the handle. Now you have a place for the plunger as well as the toilet paper!

- Or, go to a craft store and buy a paper towel holder that has been disguised as a duck, cat, dog, or whatever, and the holder is vertical (up and down) rather than horizontal (side to side). It generally holds three rolls of paper easily and you can just set the fourth on top, if you want. If you like doing crafts, you can finish a plunger yourself to match the theme of your home or bathroom.

- There are also cute craft items made specifically for toilet paper. I have one that looks just like a toilet and you have to pick up the lid to get the roll of paper out. Cute conversation piece.

- If your kids like bathtub toys, keep them in a mesh bag that either hangs from the faucet or can be adhered to the shower wall with suction cups.

- Get mesh bags for bathtub toys. Hang the mesh bag from a plastic clothes hanger on the inside of the shower rod if you keep your curtain closed. Be sure that whatever you use (toys and container), will hold up to all the water and will drain and dry out between baths.

BATHROOM CHATTER

- **Keep a spray bottle with ammonia and water (one part ammonia, four parts water) under the sink with some paper towels. Wipe the sink top and bowl every once in a while to eliminate the germs. This is also good on the toilet seat and on the mirrors.**
- **Quit scrubbing your toilet, use bleach instead. If badly stained, pour in two cups of bleach, swish (okay, scrub) with a toilet brush and let stand for a few hours. Flush again. If the toilet is still stained, repeat the process, again using the toilet brush to get at some of the stubborn areas. Once cleaned you can use one-half to one cup of bleach weekly, swish around with the toilet brush, let sit for half an hour, and voila! You have a clean toilet! I do this myself. It really works. When using bleach use caution about splashes made with the toilet brush and the "swishing" in order to preserve the color in floor mats and your clothing.**

As in any other room of your house, your options are limitless. Stop yelling, "Help, I need somebody!" look for that way yourself, and ask God to guide you. I know you can do it! Therefore . . .

Summary

- Containerize everything you possibly can using containers, drawers or baskets.
- Look for storage areas beneath the sink, on the walls, over the toilet, on the floor and on the window sill.
- Assign spaces for everyone if you're sharing this room with others.
- Color code towels.

I Will:

- look for storage space and containers to fit in these spaces;
- avoid having more than one of each type of cosmetic item;
- learn how to share this space with others and keep my stuff contained;
- look at items that I can use for storage that may not be designed specifically for the bathroom;

- keep my children safe and store all prescriptions and drinkable items out of their way;
- identify each person's towel so that I don't have to always pick up after them;
- find a hamper that will fit my bathroom and make sure that everyone knows how to use it!

Thomas Edison said, "There's a way to do it better ...find it." We're going to do just that – so hang on!

The next room is your private sanctuary – your bedroom. We're going to call this adult area of the home the master bedroom.

CHAPTER SEVEN

Bedroom Or War Zone?

A Look at Your Bedroom

The largest bedroom in a home or apartment is typically where the adults sleep. If the room is big enough, it can become a sanctuary of peace where reading or other quiet activities can take place, away from noisy children, a loud television or a blaring stereo.

Lately, for many people, the bedroom has become a home office and the pursuits of peace and calm have gone by the wayside and it has become a war zone.

The Bedroom as a Home Office

Some people use the extra space in a master bedroom to create an office. Though this may be absolutely necessary because of space requirements, a home office in a bedroom can cause difficulties. If you share the room with anyone, it's almost an impossible combination.

The bedroom should be for rest and relaxation. Search for a better place to work, even if you have to convert a long hall closet into an office and drag in some electrical lines.

The biggest problem with having an office in your bedroom is that you always see the work in front of you and you go to bed feeling guilty that you haven't accomplished what you thought you should throughout the day.

Sometimes people hide the work area with a screen. Better, but I'm not convinced. You'll have to visit with me another time to find out about home offices.

If you have a computer that you're trying to keep the kids away from and you can only do that in your bedroom, I'll relent, but I'll relent only for the computer. Your business work should be done elsewhere. You're clever. You'll find a niche to work in!

So let's pretend that you're not working in the bedroom. After all, you may have bigger concerns just finding your bed!

A Sleeping Place

The primary use of the master bedroom is as a Bedroom. The centerpiece of the room is the bed, of course. Keeping it neat and available (ready to climb in) is the best start to a clutter-free, restful room. Since you may have problems keeping your bed made, let's talk about this.

Bed Making

Making the bed can be a problem for adults, just like it is for kids. If you're frustrated with this process, then keep the bedding very simple. Buy fitted bottom sheets only. If you must use a top sheet, consider pinning it underneath the foot of the mattress.

A comforter, rather than a bedspread, is much easier to work with and still makes the bed look nice. Even the comforter can be pinned underneath the foot of the mattress, if it makes it easier for you.

To complete the picture you can just lay a pillow sham on top of your pillow and your bed is made. If you like lots of decorator pillows on your bed, be sure there's a place to put them when it's time to go to bed. The floor is not a good choice! Clutter Starts!

If you do start tossing pillows on the floor, guess what the room looks like when you don't make the bed! Have a chair or bench in your room for the pillows to go on. Encouragement: Do anything to make things easier on yourself – you're looking for clutter free, not perfection!

Many people find it "easier" not to make the bed at all! Not acceptable! The very focus of the room – the bed – is a mess this way. And when the bed's not made it makes it "easier" to toss clothes on it, and books, and papers, and...

Instead, try making your bed when you are more prone to make it. It needs to fit into your usual habits.

For instance, the only way my bed gets made every day is that I make it the minute I'm out of bed. If I dare leave the bedroom without making my bed, forget it! It doesn't get made. It took me a while to get into the habit of doing this immediately, right out of bed, but I am so glad that I did.

Someone else told me that they did it that way, so I tried it. Now I'm passing the information on to you. It won't hurt to try! By the way, when I say "try," I mean to actually do it for at least 21 days to make it a habit. If you try it for two or three days and say, "I just can't do it!," that isn't trying real hard!

A Quiet Sanctuary

Into this orderly room, where the bed is made and clothes are tucked away, we sometimes like to escape to read, think, do quiet hobbies, exercise, or generally relax. It's your sanctuary, your resting place, where...

"You will find rest for your souls." (Jeremiah 6:16)

If this is what you do now or would like to do, you'll need different supplies for your room to further this goal.

Quiet Reading

If reading is your thing, you'll need storage for your collection of books. If you like to read many books at the same time, pick an area where you can comfortably do this and be sure that you have something to hold all the books (like a basket), unless a bookcase is close enough.

However, try to keep the number of books in your bedroom to a minimum. Books collect dust and could possibly trigger allergic reactions not only to the dust but to the printing ink also. Bookcases that have glass doors (sometimes referred to as "lawyer" bookcases) might alleviate some of these problems.

If allergies are not an issue, and you really want lots of books in your bedroom, buy some sturdy bookcases and anchor them securely to the walls. This is a sleeping room so you'll be more comfortable knowing that you're safe through the night, especially if you have tall bookcases.

Safety is a real concern in earthquake country, storm-prone areas, and where children are present in the home. Tall bookcases really should not face the bed, nor be positioned where they could fall across the bed. We don't want you reclining, reading the latest romance novel, when your "little darling" climbs for the candy bar he spies on the top shelf and manages to bring the bookcases crashing down on you both.

Besides, unless you have a really large bedroom, having bookcases that are eight feet tall will make the room look really small. The best size bookcases for the bedroom are the two-shelf or three-shelf variety. Placement of the bookcases makes a difference too.

Bookcases that are too close to doors are going to take a beating. If they're too close to the opening of the bedroom, you could find yourself running into them, scuffing arms, elbows or hands as you come whipping through the door.

For reading, thinking, needlework, or listening to music, comfortable seating is necessary. Other than the bed, you'll probably need a large, roomy easy chair. Perhaps even a chaise lounge.

Placing a chaise lounge in the master bedroom, though, requires some planning. It needs to be out of the line of traffic so that you can still walk through the room. Try moving the chair around to sit at different angles. Decide what'll work best for you. Perhaps angling it away from a corner, coming directly into the room might work. Or maybe placing it in front of, or alongside, a bookcase.

It would be helpful to have some table arrangement for a reading light and space for setting down a drink or snack while sitting in the chair.

If you like the idea of the chair in your room, but not all the books, perhaps it would be a good place to read to the kids and then let them take their books back to their room. Maybe a rocker would work better for you.

What about an "oasis?" Envision your chaise lounge with a silk or live plant next to it, on the wall in front of you is a picture of the ocean, and on the little table next to the chaise is a "white noise" machine with ocean waves constantly soothing you, or the sound of rain, crickets or frogs. Just think of all the possibilities!

Other Possibilities

A woman I know uses her master bedroom as her worship center. She has her Bibles and a comfortable chair ready and waiting for her. She even has a snuggly blanket for cold days or nights. And, of course, a box of tissues.

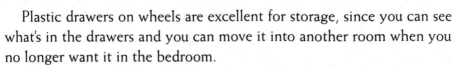

Quiet hobbies are appropriate in the master bedroom, especially if they're easily contained. Working on a collection of coins, stamps, and such is appropriate, as is sewing and needlework. Treat your hobby or sewing area like you do your reading area. Keep it out of traffic and have reasonable storage for your supplies.

Plastic drawers on wheels are excellent for storage, since you can see what's in the drawers and you can move it into another room when you no longer want it in the bedroom.

For the more energetic, the master bedroom is the ideal place to keep some exercise equipment where you can pump iron in privacy.

A friend of mine uses her bedroom as her yoga center. She uses a mat to sit on that she pulls out from beneath the bed. Collapsible exercise apparatus like rowing machines can also be slid under the bed out of the way. If enough wall space is available, multiple-station gym centers can be installed there and folded up when not in use.

Besides sleeping or resting in our bedrooms, we also get dressed in this room.

A Dressing Room

The second most important daily use for the master bedroom is as a dressing room. There are real dangers of constant clutter here, so let's talk about closets and drawers, what they're used for and what you put into them.

The Closet

Clothing is typically stored in closets and drawers. Master bedrooms often have larger closets because they are made especially for adults.

There are several types of closets. And not everyone has the luxury of a walk-in closet. Some closets have swinging doors; others have "sliders." Some have customized built-in shelving units and drawers, while others have the typical wooden or metal rod that hangs from one wall to the other and sits beneath a shelf.

Whatever your bedroom closet looks like, it helps to have it organized so that you can actually retrieve a piece of clothing without fear of getting hit on the head from a falling object!

Organizing a closet isn't difficult, but, like paperwork, it takes some time. The big difference between clothes and paper storage is that you usually don't have new items coming into a closet every day for which you need to find a home. And if you do, please call me! I must visit!

You may wonder why your closets are always a mess when you really don't intend for them to get messy. Well, does any of the following sound familiar?

- Shoe clutter – you toss one pair of shoes into the bottom of the closet because you're just too tired to bend over and put them on your shoe rack. Then another pair joins that one, and before the week is out, mates get separated and they're not visible under the hanging clothes.

- Belts, scarves and ties – you throw them over the clothes rod, loop them through a hanger or fling them onto a shelf because, again, you're too tired to figure out what to do with them. And then you quickly close the closet door so they don't fall out!

- Hats – especially the winter knit caps. You run in, take your hat off and away it goes, into the nearest open drawer or on the nearest available shelf, or on top of the dresser.

- Gloves – same story as for hats.

Okay. Now that you've looked at what you do, here's a question for you. Did you know that you probably have too many clothes? That may be difficult to admit or even to conceive possible. "You can never have too many clothes!" you say. But let me show you what I mean. I want you to go through a process with me in sorting through every single thing you wear.

That may sound like a big order, but if you take it in stages, you'll end up with a really useful wardrobe. Then we'll find ways of storing your clothes properly and conveniently so that clothes clutter will be a thing of the past. And your bedroom can become a haven again.

The reason organizing your clothes takes time is that you really have to go through all of your clothing – belts, shoes, ties, hats, gloves, jewelry – everything, to weed out items that you can no longer use or that belong elsewhere.

Before you start this process, decide how much time you have to devote to this in one day. You may think you can do it all in one day, but don't set yourself up for this. Think about doing this in one or two-hour sessions.

Usually my clients will tolerate two to three hours at a time and then call it quits. Because of this, I suggest starting this process slowly with the following steps. But first we need some tools, just like we needed when we worked in the other areas of the house.

Have several boxes ready to put items into. Label the boxes:

- Cleaning
- Altering & Repairing
- Too Small
- Too Big
- Give Away/Sell
- Throw Away.

You decide which of these you'll need. And you may need others.

So stand back! We're opening the door to the closet! Don't be embarrassed, it's just you and me – and like a doctor, I've seen it all before!

How to Sort Your Clothes

- Let's go through all of your clothing first and remove every thing you want to keep that needs cleaning or repairing. I don't want you to load up your bed, chair or floor with these items, so put them into one of two boxes labeled "Cleaning" and "Altering & Repairing."

- When we're done, these boxes will be removed from the bedroom. The "Cleaning" items can be taken to the cleaners or to your laundry area. The "Repairing' items can be taken to the seamstress, shoemaker, jeweler, or to your sewing area. (If you do sew, decide when you'll be able to fix these items so they don't linger beyond two weeks. You might write a target date for finishing the mending on the box, then write a reminder on that date on your calendar!)

- Remove all items that are to be thrown away. This is the clothing that is stained, bleached out, worn out and torn beyond repair. Put them in a "Throw Away" box. Just because you're scrubbing the toilet doesn't mean you have to look like someone who's been in the toilet! What if someone comes to the door!

- However, you might want to keep one set of clothes for wearing when you do the dirtiest jobs, such as painting or changing the oil in your car.

- You can make rags out of some discarded clothing.

- Some people use old clothing items in crafts. You can remove buttons for later use.

But don't let these tasks keep you from removing the "Throw Away" box from the bedroom. The disposal of these items should take place almost immediately to avoid cluttering up another part of the house.

- Go through your clothing again and remove items that are too big. This will probably require you to try on things if you're unsure of the fit. Definitely put them in the box marked "Too Big" if they are too big.

- Keeping items that are too big is a way of sabotaging yourself. You may as well say, "It doesn't matter if I eat the whole plate of french fries, I'll just wear my baggy pants when I can't zip the ones I'm wearing!"

- The only reason to keep oversized items is if you plan to alter them to fit. Put these in the "Altering & Repairing" box. But, again, set a deadline.

- Remove all the clothing that is too small to the "Too Small" box. You have some options here:

  (A) If you're truly on a diet and are definitely losing weight, then take these clothes to another closet. When your current clothes start getting too loose, then you can start bringing the smaller items back in (and removing the baggy ones!).

  (B) If you're not on a diet, but are keeping the clothing because you believe you'll get into them one day, put them in another closet, or fold them into a large plastic container and store them in the garage or on a shelf that you don't need to get to immediately. Use a container, label its contents and date it. If you don't wear them in two years, then it's time to give them to someone who can use them. Here again, like keeping items that are too big, you are sabotaging yourself with clothing that's too small. Every time you look at these clothes you're going to kick yourself because you can't get into them. You'll say things like, "I just have to lose five pounds and I'll fit into this," or, "I just can't give this away, I love it and it's still good," or, "This cost me a fortune, I just have to keep it!"

On occasion people do lose weight and are thrilled to be able to fit back into their "old" clothes. The operative word here is "old." Be sure to check if the style is proper before you decide to wear something in public that you bought years ago.

- Now remove items that you can give away to places like the Salvation Army or Goodwill. The "Give Away" box could include items you never wear for some reason, such as, they're uncomfortable, nothing goes with them, they're out of style, you don't like the way you look in them.

- You can probably include all or some of those items sorted into the "Too Big" and "Too Small" boxes into this box.

- All of these items should be in good, wearable condition for resale or distribution. Charities call all the time for donations and will usually come and pick up items you no longer need. They also give you a receipt which can be used for a tax deduction for charitable contributions. Later you can assign what you think is the fair market value of your clothing, so keep a list of the types of clothing you give away, for instance, blouses, slacks, shoes, etc. If these organizations don't exist in your area, contact houses of worship shelters and halfway houses to see if they have a need.

Another way of letting go of used clothing and accessories is to sell them. Put these items in a "For Sale" box. Two choices come to mind here.

- Those who like garage sales can try to sell them on a weekend either in your own yard or combined with a friend's or neighbor's sale.

- Or you can take used items to a consignment shop, to have them sold for you. You get to keep a percentage of the sale. (These are great places for selling clothing for kids since they grow so fast.) But remember, these shops feature seasonal items, so they might need to keep things until their season rolls around. Sometimes they won't accept items out of season. Sorry, you'll have to store them until the season is here.

- You may have one more step – returning clothing items that belong to someone else. The someone else can be a member of your household or a friend or relative that you borrowed that shirt from and never returned! A thorough look into your closet and drawers sometimes brings to light some interesting surprises! Have a box available for these also.

Hey, guess what? You're done! Now we can tackle all the other stuff – the belts, ties, shoes, scarves, purses, etc., that are scared to death you're coming after them – and rightly so because we're going to take a close look at them also! (We will arrange all of these items, later in this chapter?)

We'll start our next tackle job on your shoes. Neat shoe storage is very important. Depending on how many shoes you own, their storage place can vary.

Shoes

You can leave your shoes in their original boxes and put them on the closet shelf, preferably with labels so you know the contents, or you can buy shoe racks or shoe bins that hang from the back of a door, on walls, or on the floor in the closet.

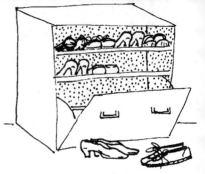

If you have built-in shelves in your closet, you can put your shoes there. There are also shoe "cases." These look like low chests of drawers, but they have a front panel that tilts forward to reveal your shoes.

Let's get started by looking at your shoes. As you take each pair out of the closet, ask yourself the following questions:

- Are you wearing every pair? Repeat after me: I will not lie to myself, I will not lie to myself, I will not lie to myself. Now, remove those not worn and either put them in the trash or in the give away box.

- Do they need to be repaired or polished? Put them in the repair box.

- Are they comfortable? If not, put them in the give away box to donate or to sell.

- Are they still in style and do they go with your clothing? If not, you know what to do!

The next big item, for us ladies, are purses. Every shape, every color, and every size just to be sure that we have the right purse for just the right occasion! Let's check it out.

Purses

- Are you using every purse often enough to feel that you must keep it?

- If you're not sure, put the purse aside. You may want to put it with the other items that you're going to put someplace else for awhile to see if you really want/need it.

- Are your purses still good looking? If they have tears, stains, rips, ink marks that won't come out, then it's time to give away or discard.

- Are your purses still in style and match shoes or clothing? If not, get that box!

Sometimes it's best to invest in a neutral colored expensive purse that you can use throughout the winter and a different colored one for the summer so that you don't have to have every shade and shape on the market cluttering up your closet and drawers.

As with purses, try to limit the number of evening bags that you have. One black, one silver and one gold will generally cover all occasions. If you socialize a great deal, then adding a pearl or beaded white one to the mix may help without having every assorted type available. Evening bags can be kept nice by putting them into a plastic bag or shoe box.

An item that goes along with shoes and purses are gloves, especially in the winter. Whether you use knit mittens or gloves or leather gloves, your storage options can be the same:

Gloves

- Keep the gloves with the coat you wear them with.
- Put them all in a plastic zip-lock bag or clear shoe box. You can keep this in the closet with your clothes, or where your coats are.
- If your gloves need repairing, you know the box!

Let's not forget about your hats. You may use such a variety of hats that I'm going to stay general with my suggestions for them.

Hats

- Baseball caps can be stacked on a closet shelf or hung from specially made hangers that attach to a wall. If you're a cap collector I know that I'm not going to convince you to give any away. Display them proudly and be sure that they're all clean and nice looking.
- Berets can also be stacked neatly on a closet shelf. However, they will get dusty so I suggest that you buy a clear plastic container for them to go into.
- Many of the items that you have for winter – hats, scarves, gloves – can be put into a plastic container that goes underneath the bed. That way everything is together when you want it. If you have a lot of winter items to store when out of season, then it'll probably be better if you get the larger plastic containers that you can stack in the garage or basement.

- Picture hats are hard to store. These are the wide–brimmed hats that romance movies are filled with and also hats that gardeners love. These will store best in the larger plastic containers in the garage as closet shelves are usually too narrow for them. You can also try putting them on hooks on your bedroom wall. With pictures around they can look pretty whimsical. Try some of those pictures that show white wicker furniture, or old-fashioned type scenes. It really does look cute.
- Fedora hats are easily stackable on closet shelves. Put some plastic wrap over them and you won't have to worry about dust.

Yet another item to worry about are your scarves. They don't stack well, they don't hang well and you can never find one when you need one. Let's see if we can find some solutions for you.

CLEVER OPEN STORAGE
Gain storage by using your walls. If you wear hats, hang them on the wall. You can also hang scarves. If you're at all creative, you can make this arrangement a blend of colors and shapes that looks like it was designed that way on purpose.

Scarves
- For short scarves, fold in half and lay in a dresser drawer in a long container or put into a small clear plastic box on a shelf.
- For long dress scarves, fold lengthwise and hang over a hanger that has felt or foam on it so the scarves don't slide off. You may need more than one hanger, depending on the number of scarves you have.
- Scarves can also be hung from wall hangers that have pegs attached.
- Winter knit scarves are safe to wrap around the neck of a hanger with your coat.
- When winter is over you can put these scarves with the gloves and other winter items that are under your bed or in the garage/basement.

Do you have problems finding a belt to wear? Do you then have problems figuring out what to do with the belt? Let's go exploring:

Belts

Are you wearing every belt? Or do you have a collection that goes back to your first date, or your first job? Come on, dig them out and really look at them.

- Can you find the belt you want when you want it?

- There are many different hangers for these items so that it becomes almost a personal preference which one to buy. Look in stores like Target, Bed, Bath & Beyond, Linens 'N Things, or The Container Store, for these hangers. You can find hangers that go on the closet rod, attach to the wall, or hang from a door. If you're not sure what will work, buy it, keep your receipt and take it back if you don't like it. You don't have to make the perfect choice every time you are trying to find a solution to a problem area. Use the item for at least a week before you decide if it will work or not.

- You can hang a number of belts on a hanger. Just remember that every time you want a belt that's not on top you'll have to pull all the other ones off. Clutter Start!

- There are hangers that are made for scarves (which totally wrinkles the scarf!) but is great for holding belts. Just slide the belt through the hole and the buckle catches at the opening. If the belt and buckle are really thin, this won't work.

- Do all your belts fit? If you've been poking extra holes into the beginning or ending of the belt, well, it's time to give them away. Remember, don't sabotage yourself!

- Do any of your belts need repairing? If so, is it worth it?

We're almost through. Yea! One more item to look at – ties.

Ties

- Are you wearing every tie? Or, like your belts do you have the tie you wore on your first date, or your first job? Remove the ones you're not wearing. Give away or sell.

- Are your ties in style? Is this the year for skinny ties, or fat ties? Only keep ties that are out of current style if they are basic classic ties and you know you'll wear them again! Don't make me come back in five years and still see these hanging around and not worn! Put them in the give away box.

- Are your ties stained? Come on, you do eat, don't you? Get them cleaned right after you've stained them. If the stain doesn't come out, give it away.

We'll soon be looking at where you'll be putting your clothing in the closet, but let's first look at what we can use the shelves for.

- Closet shelves can be used for storage of foldable items like sweaters and scarves, and bulky items like hats and purses.

- Most closets have lots of wasted space above the permanent shelf. You can choose to put up another permanent shelf, or you can place plastic shelves on top of the built-in shelf so that the upper region of the closet is utilized.

- Or you can buy plastic storage bins that will stack easily and fit just the depth of the shelf. Since their contents are hidden, be sure to label these storage bins so that you know what's inside.

- Shelves, especially the higher ones, are often used for off-season items.

- Off-season items can also be stored on the floor of the closet in bins, but be absolutely sure that these off-season items don't interfere with finding and removing your in-season clothes. (If you're in a wheel chair and your clothes are hanging on lower rods, then putting bins beneath the clothing is a poor choice.)

The one area we haven't touched on yet are your dresser drawers. Yep, 'fraid so, gotta go there!

Dresser Drawers

Before we go any further, open your top dresser drawer. You're going to have to do it sooner or later so you may as well do it now.

How many stretched out, torn and disgusting items of whatever are lurking in this drawer? I don't usually say this, but throw them away!! And please don't tell me how comfortable they are and that they're now just broken in, etc., etc. Just get rid of them! Treat yourself like an important person instead of a junkyard dog. Now, let's get down to business.

Important Question: Are you a packer, or a thrower? Go ahead – guess!

Well, a packer is someone who folds and neatly stacks their underwear, pajamas, nightgowns, sweaters, socks, hosiery and any other items they want in their dresser.

A thrower? Well, I think you can guess that one. Just open up a drawer – and throw! Being a thrower isn't any better or any worse than being a packer, but it does take some discipline to make it easier for you.

If you get confused about which drawer something is in, even though you've been in it a hundred times, label the front of the drawer, or attach some pictures to remind you of what's inside. Pictures and labels help both ADD and dyslexic's find what they're looking for fairly easily.

So, if you like to throw items into a drawer because folding them drives you crazy, then at least have a drawer for different items. For instance, ladies:

- put bras and panties in one drawer; have a container in the drawer for each so that you can at least reach in and grab what you want without throwing what you don't want over your shoulder and onto the floor;
- the containers can be shoe boxes, plastic boxes, silverware holders, or anything else that you might find that is low enough and wide enough to handle your belongings. Take measurements of the drawer before buying something. Measure front-to-back and side-to-side, in addition to the height;
- put socks and hosiery in another drawer. Again, have a container for each;
- put nightgowns in another drawer. If you also use pajamas, put them in another drawer, or see if a container for each will work as you may have too many to have both in the same drawer;
- if you keep sweaters in your dresser, it's best that they have their own drawer. If you insist on throwing these into the drawer you're going to have wrinkles. Try to roll the sweaters before you put them away. At least when you open the drawer you'll be able to immediately see which sweater you want.

And for the men:

- put your underwear in one container and your T-shirts in another. If you have too many for one drawer, use one drawer for each;
- if you use pajamas, use one full drawer. You may even want to put the bottoms in one container and the tops in another;
- put your dress socks in one drawer and have a container for each dif ferent color;
- put your athletic socks in a drawer by themselves.

And for the rest of you who are packers, here are some options for you:

- if you wear outer T-shirts more than you wear dress shirts, or blouses, then hang up the T-shirts and put the dress shirts/blouses in the drawers, especially if there is not enough hanging space in the closet;

- but if you want to keep the T-shirts in the drawers, fold them so that they can stand on end, rather than lying on top of each other. This will let you quickly see and choose the shirt you want to wear;

- folding the clothing that goes into drawers so that they stand on end is a great time saver, and a space saver. You'll find that you can fit more into the drawers when clothes are upright than when they lie on top of one another;

- T-shirts, underwear, socks, pajamas, nightgowns, and sweaters are all good candidates to stand on end. This totally eliminates the need to pick up everything to see what's beneath, which usually leaves your drawers in a big mess!

Now that you've gone through all your wearing apparel in your closet and drawers, you're left with what you can really wear and enjoy. Yes, you got rid of those shoes that you really can't walk in. I know, they really did look nice and were perfect if you didn't have to walk and could just sit. But did that ever really happen? Even if you were just going out to dinner, you still had to get from the bus, car or cab into the restaurant, and then to your table. Did you like limping? And your feet aren't going to change. So bid the shoes a fond farewell. Someone else will enjoy them. You never did.

Come along, we now get to put things away so that tomorrow you know where to find what you want to wear.

Making Order out of What Is Left

You've already done the most time consuming job – sorting, deciding, crying, getting mad, throwing out, etc., etc. In general, getting rid of things that have been hanging around for years. Don't you feel lighter? Don't you even feel on the verge of feeling marvelous?

What you put back into your closet and dresser drawers could be most anything, but typically it consists of hanging clothes, shoes, purses, hats, clothing accessories, and folded clothing.

Arranging Your Clothes

There are different ways that you can hang your clothes – by the neck with a noose – No, No, Not Serious! But different ways that may make it easier for you to reach in and get what you want. Try some of the following suggestions so that you'll enjoy taking your clothes in and out of the closet because every piece of clothing will have its place.

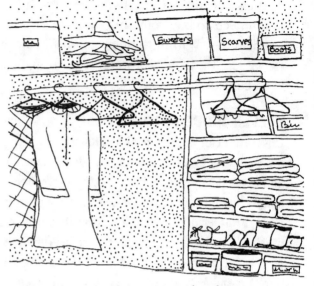

You're going to make some easy decisions right now, so that hanging things up at the end of the day will not require much effort and the guess work will be taken out of retrieving clothes in the morning. Sound like a miracle? It works like one, be assured!

You will now be grouping your clothing in some kind of logical order, and there are options for this process, too.

You can merge your clothes all together – that is, you don't care if you have a white blouse for work hanging next to a white polo shirt because they're all white.

Or, you can choose to group your clothes by the way you use them – that is, all of your work clothes in a specific area of the closet, then casual clothes, then your dressy clothes.

Let's suppose that you've decided to merge them. For instance, hang all your slacks together, whether for work or play, it doesn't matter. Do the same for your skirts, shirts, jackets, then dresses. Next, if you wish, arrange your slacks according to color – all black, all beige, all brown, etc. Do the same for your blouses, shirts, skirts and jackets.

It will be easier if you follow the same color sorting for everything that you're hanging in the closet. The purpose of grouping this way is to let you see what colors you generally wear and to make it easier for you to mix and match them.

It also becomes clear if you have too many shirts of the same color, or if you need to buy something for the slacks you can't wear because nothing matches. Within these groupings you can even group your shirts by sleeve length. If this is too tedious or nit-picky for you, then please don't even consider it.

CLEVER HIDDEN STORAGE

Off-season clothes, seasonal bed linens, or bulky sports clothing can be hidden away cleverly by using a large, plastic garbage can with wheels. Remove the lid and cover the opening with a purchased wooden round table top that is approximately one inch all around larger than the opening. You can then put a tablecloth, sheet, or other decorative throw over the wooden top. Place a lamp or vase on top of it and you have storage, plus a table. While this plastic garbage can can be used in the bedroom, the technique can be used in a hallway, the living room or family room. Actually, wherever you might need a decorative side table.

If you have chosen to separate your clothing into groups – that is, all work clothes together, then all casual clothes together and then all play clothes together – then store them the same way, by color, as we did above.

Putting it to Work

Now, put your arrangement to work. If you're a woman, and if you wear only dresses to work, you can easily rotate them by putting the cleaned dresses "behind" the ones you haven't worn yet. If you have ten dresses, you will have two work weeks of dresses in rotation, and you won't have to worry about wearing the same dress too often.

The same can apply to all your articles of clothing, from blouses to slacks. Men can rotate their sports jackets in this way, too, varying their wardrobe daily.

Next, look at the other items stored in your closet. Shoes can be arranged by color, as can scarves, ties, purses, and hats. Sweaters lying on the shelf can be arranged by type and/or color.

This storing system also gives you an idea where to place your clothes and other items when putting them away. They have a specific slot in your whole closet system where you can return them.

We're finally done in your bedroom! Wow! Look at how great everything looks. You didn't think it was possible, did you? Told ya so!

Summary

- Avoid using your bedroom as an office.
- Make bed making simple by using fitted sheets and comforters.
- If reading is a passion, make your bedroom a quiet haven with the right chair and bookcase for this purpose.
- If hobbies are your passion, make space for them by using clever storage areas.
- Weed out clothing and accessories that you no longer use from the closet and dresser drawers.
- Look inside your closets and dresser drawers to see how much space you have available for storing and hanging clothing items.
- Decide if you're a packer or thrower so that you know how to work with your dresser drawers.

Whatever you do with your bedroom, remember that everything in it needs a home. So if you have lots of books, earnestly strive to get them put back on the shelf.

Also work at putting your clothes away every night in the closet, drawers, or in the laundry hamper, and stow your shoes, ties and belts in their homes so they're easier to find next time. While you're doing that, you can decide what you'll wear tomorrow.

It's been a tough job, but you made it through. Now you can say:

I Will:

- not have an office in my bedroom;
- make my bed every day on my best schedule;
- make my bedroom my sanctuary where I can do what I want to do – and will bring in supplies so that I can do whatever that might be;
- faithfully go through all of my clothing items and keep only those items that I wear regularly;
- store clothing that I think I may wear in the future, but if I don't wear it within a two year period of time I will give it away.

And now, have a restful night!

"My people will abide in a peaceful habitation, in secure dwellings, and in quiet resting places." (Isaiah 32:18)

Now, be brave, for we're going into the children's room! Don't worry, I'm still here!

CHAPTER EIGHT

Creepy Crawlers

Children and Growing

Children are special little people trying to grow up to be big people. We have to go slow with them. In a sense, we have to show them how to "crawl" before we teach them how to "walk."

It takes confidence at the very first step to get them to take the second step. If they fall, they need to know that it isn't the end of the world.

One fall (hurdle) that children deal with is self-esteem (respect for self), which leads to self-confidence (reliance on self). And they need this emotional strength to survive and mature into capable adults.

Unfortunately, among other signs of low self-esteem is a painfully obvious one – clutter. People who have homes and offices that are cluttered seem to say, "I don't like me or anyone else who shares this space." Although grown, these adults are still little kids.

All children benefit from a healthy dose of self-esteem. For the child with Attention Deficit Disorder or a learning disability, self-esteem and self-confidence are a must. If children with ADD/LD learn to conquer their home environment, this strength can then bolster them in the external environment.

In addition for these children, frustration comes rapidly when what they want to find, do or accomplish just isn't happening for them.

Let's try to make it possible for them to be successful at this early stage. We'll go through a step-by-step process to help kids when they need to make choices in life by setting parameters.

Typically, we guide children, train them, nurture them and feed them. Then we need to let them "Fly Free." As it's written,

"Train up a child in the way he should go and when he is old, he will not depart from it."
(Proverbs 22:6)

Let's start looking at how we can help ourselves to help our children in the areas that they have to conquer, beginning at their birth and working through the teens. As in other rooms, all items will have a home where they belong. Remind your children of this as they grow so it becomes a habit.

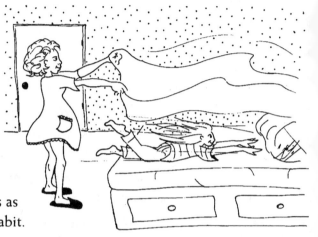

The New Baby

Congratulations! You've brought your dimpled darling home. Since you'll be in complete charge of this child for a good year, you may have to deal with a crib, a changing table, rocker, chest of drawers, toy chest, etc.

And of course we can't forget the diapers, sleepers, T-shirts, tops, bottoms, blankets and whatever else you can think of.

Let's start with the three most essential pieces of furniture first:

- a bed, because babies sleep (sometimes);
- a changing table, because they mess their diapers (always);
- and a rocking chair, because they cry and nurse (almost always).

The Bed

The first essential item is the bed. Well, he needs a place to sleep. Although my baby slept in a dresser drawer for two months before we had a crib given to us, a crib is nice because you can remove the mattress later and use it on a toddler bed when the baby gets older.

Be sure the crib you use is safe so that the baby can't get his head stuck between the bars (ouch!), or have the adjustable railing suddenly drop when baby tries to stand up. That's not a great confidence booster to try and stand up and instead go flipping over the railing as it slides down! In addition to the safety of the crib, you'll need to consider the safe placement of the crib. When children start climbing, they'll climb anything, so keep the crib away from windows, dressers, doors and light fixtures.

The Changing Table

Having a dresser right away is really not necessary, but if you don't have a changing table, then you can use a dresser top:

- pad the top with blankets so that it's soft;

- cover the blankets with a leakproof pad;

- cover the leakproof pad with a sheet or receiving blanket.

I highly recommend that if you use a dresser as a changing table, that you buy a rail guard so that the baby cannot roll off (just in case you're trying to reach for a diaper and have to turn your back on the rambunctious little tyke).

The Rocker

A rocker is also recommended because it can be soothing for both you and baby and if he has a bad night you'll really appreciate it! The rocking seems to comfort babies back to sleep. Or so we hope!

Once your baby is sleeping through the night and old enough to start crawling, I suggest that you move the rocker to another room and try to keep the baby's room clear of obstacles. Afterall, getting around the toys will be challenging enough. And speaking of toys...

The Toy Chest and Other Storage Areas

Sometimes relatives load you down with toys that the baby obviously can't play with for two or three years. And there's just too many to keep out in the open in the baby's room. So what do you do with all that stuff?

- Load up the toy chest with excess toys and put the toy chest in the closet. (When you don't have toys to worry about, use the chest for other storage until it's needed.)

- Little bicycles or cars that don't fit into the toy chest can also be put into the closet.

- If you get tons of stuffed toys for the baby and you've run out of room in the toy chest, there are mesh nets that function like a hammock. It fits at a corner and attaches to each wall.

- Don't hang this over the crib because sooner or later your little darlin' will figure out how to climb to it.

- And, until the child's old enough to walk and climb, having a rocking horse in the room is a cute touch, but not necessary.

- For safety sake, keep the rocking horse in your sight when the child's on it, or wants to be on it. That may mean that the horse lives in the living room awhile, but didn't I hear you say something the other day about "it looks like a bunch of animals live here?"

The Baby's Room

Sometimes the baby's room has been a guest room or an office, so the closets are full of "stuff." Or the room has to be shared rather than baby having it all to himself.

If the baby's room is going to be a shared room – with either another child or an adult using it as an office – divide the closet as soon as possible, keeping half of it for the baby – you'll soon need it.

If baby is sharing the room with another child, then dividing the closet now is better than waiting for later when the arguments start. (See section below on "Sharing Rooms.")

Besides the baby's bed and her toys, there are also other items that you'll need for her. Lets start with diapers and clothing.

Diaper Bags: One item that you absolutely want to have on hand is a traveling diaper bag. Whether this is an actual diaper bag, or a tote that you use as a diaper bag doesn't matter. As long as the bag allows for diapers, bottles, wipes, food and playthings you'll be fine.

For at-home use, diapers and clothing for your baby can be easily handled with diaper bags – not the kind you take with you, but the kind that can hang. These bags hold lots of diapers and if you get two of them, the second one can hold the little T-shirts and socks.

Clothing: If you have a multitude of baby clothes, then you'll need a chest of drawers. However, you can also put these clothes into open plastic bins beneath the crib. When your child starts to crawl and gets curious, transfer the clothes into a plastic container with a tight fitting lid. This container will probably fit beneath the crib also.

If you get dresses for the baby, buy some of the small hangers and put the dresses in the closet. If there's no room, you can buy a small "chiffarobe" as one client did.

Hannah

Hannah had two other children who had to share their room with the new baby. The closets were taken over with the older children's clothes, as was the one chest of drawers. She and her husband decided to buy a second-hand "closet" or chiffarobe, a combination wardrobe and chiffonier. This piece of furniture has drawers down the left side with a shelf near the top and on the right is a closed compartment that has a clothes rod in it,  and thus the "closet." All the baby's clothes went into that chiffarobe and was used by that child for many years.

When the baby starts to outgrow those cute little clothing items, you either have to give them away or store them to be handed down. Try to be reasonable here. If the new baby is your first child and you plan on more, then storing is probably a safe thing to do. However, if you already have all boys and this baby is a girl and future children look like a slim chance, then storing is probably not the best solution.

If you choose to store them, be sure to wash them and remove all stains before putting them away or these clothes are really going to smell when you open the box. Where do you store them?

- If you have room on the closet shelf, you can box these items into cardboard boxes.

- Shoe boxes will work for saving the shoes and socks.

- Be sure to label what's inside the boxes and the sizes.

- Labeling applies to larger boxes as well.

- Try not to mix different sizes, or seasons, in one box. Example: don't mix baby underwear, size 0 with winter dresses, size 6 months or summer slacks, size one year, etc.

- If you have only a few items to save, it's best to still keep these separate. You can put them into large plastic baggies and then transfer them into a large plastic container with a tight fitting lid.

- You can store these items in a garage or storage shed, but put them in plastic containers as mice, roaches and silverfish love cardboard. Put some cedar chips in with the clothes to keep any bug away. And this certainly smells nicer than moth balls!

Furniture for the Maturing Child

We've covered your baby's room, and his/her clothing, so let's take a look now at room furniture for when s/he starts to mature.

Floor Sleepers

The simplest sleeping furniture for your young child just out of his/her crib might possibly be a mattress on the floor with some bedding. Some children refuse to sleep in a bed, and some parents find that the mattress on the floor is only a "phase" before their child feels ready to being up higher in a regular framed bed.

It's possible that the desire to sleep on the floor is less risky for a child who may fear falling out of bed. There's no harm in letting them sleep on a mattress on the floor, so make it fun. Put the mattress inside a pup tent, making it an adventure for him. On the tent use a theme design they like, and if you can afford it, follow the theme into the room.

As an alternative, string a rope across the room and put a blanket across it, making a "pseudo" tent over the mattress. Then tuck the blanket edges under the sides of the mattress. Some Moms use the blanket approach because their child's ideas change from week to week about how to sleep. Use posters, cutouts, contact paper, or even their drawings to hang on the "walls" of this tent. If you're talented, make curtains and table skirts of the same theme.

The mattress bed can also be used as a mini-couch by putting it against a wall and arranging an assortment of small pillows on it, matching the theme, of course! The cover can be a sheet or blanket that matches the pillows.

Unless your child likes to sleep on the floor, and you have arranged for a comfy way to do that, your child will need a bed. Since I don't sell furniture, I can only recommend bedding in general terms.

Bed Sleepers

Once your child is out of a crib, the crib mattress can be moved to a small toddler bed frame. These bed frames can be found in most department, furniture and variety stores. They are fairly inexpensive and should be big enough until the child is five or six, depending on their size.

A twin comforter will work in this toddler bed if laid sideways. The longer part can be tuck under the mattress nearest the wall side so it can't be seen when you walk into the room. You can still use crib sheets, of course, however, these sheets don't come with top sheets, so a twin sheet will have to be used.

You can also put that sheet sideways if you wish, also tucking the excess under the mattress. If you can machine sew a straight seam, cut a twin bed sheet in half and finish the raw edges. You now have two toddler bed top sheets. Or buy yard goods in juvenile patterns being sure that the sheet is long enough to tuck in at the end of the bed. Just turn the raw edges twice and sew. Flannel is nice for cold months.

Once your sweetie is ready to move out of the small bed, you need to decide if the room is large enough for a twin, double, queen or king bed. If you're going to opt for a larger-than-twin bed, buy something that you know will last well into their late teen years. Think about all the jumping and "plopping" that beds have to endure. Sometimes buying an inexpensive but sturdy twin bed is better until the child grows out of the trampoline stage!

Beds are available in particle board, solid wood, or metal. There are even some plastic models around. One of the things to pay attention to when buying beds is what the edges are like and how they're connected. Are there sharp edges or fittings that may cut your child when they do the triple flip off the bed? Trust me, rushing your child to the hospital with a cut head is definitely not fun!

Some beds are built on platforms and offer drawers beneath the bed. If you have limited space in the room, this might be a good option, especially if you buy a "bookcase" headboard with it. Other beds have extenders on the headboard that attach to a desk. Again, check the edges and fittings for anything sharp.

Bunkbeds are obvious when you have children sharing a room. I prefer that the younger child decide which bed they want to sleep in, because of Jeremy.

Jeremy

A young child terrified of being in the lower bunk because he thought his older brother would come crashing down on top of him. The older one didn't care where he slept so he got the lower bunk and made a fortress out of it by hanging blankets on all sides from the underside of the top bunk. And of course, the younger child was not allowed into this private domain!

At any rate, there are bunkbeds that also have a desk space available beneath the upper bunk, while the lower bunk is off to the side at a ninety-degree angle. It takes away from the total stacked bunkbed look.

Speaking of desks, they generally are a good item to have in your child's room. They need a quiet place to study and play.

Desk Area

What kind of desk you choose may depend on the amount of space in the room. If you really have limited space, consider the twin bed that sits on a platform above the desk area. The child has to be old enough to master the ladder to the bed, however. This desk/bed option makes good use of wall space and also offers a small bookcase on one side of the platform.

- With any desk you choose, you need to decide on the type of material the desk should be made of (wood, metal, plastic) and what features each affords.

- Check the drawers to be sure that they move easily and won't fall out onto the floor.

- Brightly colored plastic desks usually have no drawers, so the rolling carts with drawers might be an option here, placed beneath the table.

- A regular folding table can also be used as a desk, if you get a sturdy one. The inexpensive ones wobble too much.

- An advantage to the folding table is that it can be folded and put away, if necessary, or used someplace else.

Another item to consider in this room is a bookcase if one doesn't come with another piece of furniture, like the bunkbed/desk set.

Bookcases

I recommend a small two-shelf bookcase, which can sit on the floor, or even be attached to the wall. Again, these shelves can be wood, plastic or metal.

If you're going to get a tall bookcase, anchor it to the wall, so that if it's climbed by "Jungle Jim" or "Annie Oakley," it won't come crashing down. And if you live in earthquake country, you definitely want to anchor a tall bookcase to the wall.

Whatever you put into a child's room, be safety conscious. Watch for sharp edges, edges that stick out, and things that can fall over or fall down. We need to take care of our precious little cargo.

With the furniture taken care of, we can now move on to training this precious cargo in matters of clothing.

Clothing

Getting dressed often creates nightmares for both you and your child. When children are first able to dress themselves, they are only concerned with getting the clothing on, so choices aren't usually necessary. You can just give them what they need. But when they start saying, "No, I don't want to wear that," then that's the time to start offering another choice of clothing. To help your children gain self-confidence with dressing, offer graduated options in clothing to keep things simple.

Options

When trying to teach a very young child about options in clothing, start by offering them only two choices. For instance, as you're holding up two tops, say "You can wear all blue today, or you can wear all yellow, which would you like?"

In an article entitled "The Blame Game," in the February 2000 Reader's Digest, written by Libby Lucas from Toronto Life Fashion (December/January '98), Lee Ann Russell, a teacher and guidance counselor, agrees with making choices.

Russell states, "Parents should start by letting kids make choices. Ask if they want to wear the blue pajamas or the yellow ones. Then don't let them change their minds. You have to start living with the consequences of your decisions early, so you'll learn from your mistakes and make better choices." And we don't even know each other! We even chose the same colors to use as examples!

It's also best to use solid colors to start with and then gradually bring in patterns. Then the option would be whether they want to wear a patterned top with solid bottoms, vice versa, or wear a top and bottom that is all solid colors.

You could try the following if you run into problems that a client used with success.

LeAnn

LeAnn's children were changing their clothes a minimum of three times a day. Well, with four children that creates a considerable amount of laundry. At my urging, she took ALL of their clothing away and handed them, daily, what they were to wear all day. They stopped complaining in about a week so she then started the graduated process, giving them only one of two choices. They soon graduated to three choices, and so forth. I also recommended that she limit their choices to among seven outfits, but one outfit per day. Too many choices overwhelm little kids. They need to have restraints until they mature and feel confident about their choices. (Of course, we're not much better at this when we stand in front of our closets with clearly more than seven choices! And we're supposed to be mature!)

Speaking of maturity, let's look at how we can help this process.

Levels of Maturity

Maturing will be different from one child to the next. But if you give them access to all their clothes at one time, and say, "Go get dressed," you'll have **Clutter Start!**

They'll go into their drawers and literally fling clothes out of the drawer until they find something they think they'd like to wear. They need to learn how to make choices before they can be "let loose" in the chest of drawers. Your saying, "What you pick is what you'll be wearing all day, unless I decide you need to change your clothes" will help them learn to make wise choices.

Another help here is to have only seven outfits for each child, (7 tops, 7 bottoms, and possibly 7 dress-up items). This helps them, but it also helps you. Since most people do laundry at least once a week, the seven outfits should be enough.

Getting used to wearing seven different outfits may possibly avoid the adult result of having a closet full of clothes with "nothing to wear." (You can have the children feel special by letting them wear a dress-up item on wash day if they truly have only seven outfits and you wash every seven days.) It also simplifies shopping for clothing; you'll easily see when something needs to be replaced. Another problem associated with dressing is looking for socks and underwear.

Calling All Socks!

Your child is wearing blue for the day, so he wants to find the blue socks, but can't. An option is to purchase only white socks in order to avoid scrambling for a matching colored pair.

Or you can "colorize" each small child, as discussed in "Sharing Rooms," later. Try to have only seven to ten pairs of socks at a time, for the same laundry and shopping reasons as mentioned above.

- If your children are close in size, sew a single colored thread near the toe that lets the child know the socks are his. If the thread "freaks them out," take a permanent marker and put their initial on the bottom of the sock.

- If you are lucky enough to have these socks last long enough to be handed down, you will have to cross out the old initial, or just add the new initial next to the old.

The same philosophy applies to underwear and outerwear, which can be marked on the labels. Clothing and underwear are not the only things that cause headaches for children. "Little things" can become monsters for them.

"Little" Things

Avoid buttons, ties and straps that add frustration to your child's dressing time. In order for them to gain self-esteem and confidence, they need to have success.

Constantly failing at trying to button something when they're in a hurry doesn't add much to the self-confidence necessary to master this feat. If this is a problem, replace the buttons, etc., with snaps, hooks and eyes, or velcro.

- If your child uses hair ribbons, elastic hair bands, barrettes, belts and shoe laces, these items need a "home," a place where they can always be found without a lot of jumping up and down and screaming. The home can be a thing or place that makes it easy for children to take care of themselves.

- A toilet paper roll can be a holder for the elastic hair bands, which is then placed on a dresser top, in a dresser drawer, or in a bathroom drawer.

- Barrettes and clips can be put into a plastic container that sits on a dresser top, inside a dresser drawer, or bathroom drawer.

- Hair ribbons can be draped over a small dowel type stand (like a coffee cup holder) or a dowel type wall hanging (the accordion type one that stretches and can also be used for coffee cups).

If the ribbons are put into a container or drawer, they may become tangled or lose their neat appearance, causing more time to unknot them or iron them, and your kid is jumping up and down again because she's late for school but MUST wear that particular hair ribbon.

- Belts are another problem. If there are many, they take up a lot of space. You can hang them from hangers, on a hook inside the closet, or on a wall holder.

The problem with the wall holder is that the hooks are rather thick and some belt buckles are not wide enough to go over them. Some stores sell "scarf" organizers, which I personally use for my belts. I find that the opening wrinkles the scarves, but a belt slips right into the hole and the belt buckle keeps it from falling out.

If the belt buckle is too small, I just drape the belt through the hole. This holder is made out of plastic, has 28 openings, and hangs from a clothes rod, just like a hanger. This is also a good solution for hair ribbons. Scarves will wrinkle on this holder, hair ribbons would not, and it would be fairly easy to slip the ribbon through the hole.

- Shoe laces, if there are many, can also be draped through this type of holder, or over dowels on a wall hanging. A few can be put into a plastic holder, similar to the holder for barrettes. Small plastic bins can also be used for all these small items; even a kitchen silverware holder can be used. Just decide how much room you need and where your child wants these items to be accessible. Accessibility is also a problem when it comes to shoes.

Shoes

Shoes are always a problem. Kids come in the door and off go the shoes. Sometimes they may even get to their rooms before they kick them off. The following will help you through this.

- Keep a plastic bin with a lip on it (the type used for vegetables), or a large basket, near the door they usually use.

When next they kick off their shoes, have them pick them up and put them in the basket. If they don't, you do it – once. Tell them that they'll have to pay to get their shoes back if they continue to just kick them off in the "communal" living areas. Set whatever you feel is a fair fee to retrieve the shoes. If they have no money, take it out in labor!

- If you don't like having the shoes at the front door, then think about having a bin or basket available in their room.

- In the closet in their rooms you can put either a floor shoe rack, or a small shelf or bookcase for the shoes.

- Also available for shoes are mesh bags that hang on doors, or walls.

- There are also rolling flat racks that fit beneath the bed that shoes go onto. The shoes usually wind up hidden beneath the bed, so why not have a rack available to catch them?

Take your child with you when buying these items so they can tell you which one they would most likely use. By the way, before they even say anything, tell them that the floor is not an option!

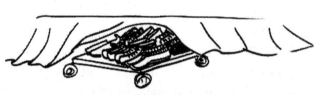

The whole idea is to make it easy for the kids to get at their own things and also to return things to where they got them from. Training, training, training. Yes, it takes time to train, but the rewards are Wonderful! Now, onto more training items.

Using Chests of Drawers/Closets

Some children do not take to putting their clothes away in a chest of drawers. This is especially true for kids with ADD. They can't see inside, so therefore whatever's inside doesn't exist. For kids with dyslexia, they know the clothes exist, they just can't remember which drawer it's in.

If this is true for your children, try this: take their clothes out of the drawers and put them into plastic cubbies (bins) that you can sit on top of the dresser. (If this is too high for them, place on a low table, or the floor.) If possible, put the chest in the closet.

Utilize the unused chest of drawers for toys. The kids won't complain about opening the drawers to find a toy! And if you have more than one child sharing a room, you can assign a drawer or drawers for each child's toys. Again, if you can get the chest of drawers inside the closet, it'll make the room look less cluttered.

Use one of the plastic bins for each item of clothing they don't want in the drawers, i.e., socks, underwear, shoes, tops, slacks, etc. Cut out pictures of these items from magazines, or draw them, and attach to different colored construction paper, along with the words for the picture. Then tape the pieces of paper to the outside of the cubbies.

This is really educational, and gives them three lessons in one. How to recognize

1) colors,

(2) pictures and

3) words.

If you need several cubbies and there's not enough room on top of the chest of drawers, try a folding table instead.

If you have a child with dyslexia, and they want their clothes to remain in the dresser drawers, try putting pictures on the outside of the drawers. Be careful that the picture's not too explicit in case your child has friends over that might make fun of the pictorial guides.

Clothes can be wrinkled when using a cubbie or basket system, so keep their good clothes hung up. Speaking of hung up, if you want the children to hang up their clothes themselves, lower the clothes rod so the shortest child can reach it. Imagine what it would be like if you had to hang up your clothes in a closet where the rods are ten feet high!

If you don't like the kids putting their clothes into cubbies, or baskets, then it will be best for each child to have their own chest of drawers so that each article can have its own drawer, i.e., one for underwear, one for tops, one for pants, etc. Since children are really averse to folding, a single drawer for each of these items will create less wrinkling.

Two options that can replace conventional chests of drawers are rolling carts that have either wire baskets or plastic drawers.

- The wire baskets are visible front to back and side to side, but are really quite open. If you or your child has a problem with dust, these open bins can create some concern for dust accumulating on the clothes.

- The plastic drawers are closed all around, but because they are clear plastic the kids can see through them, so they don't quite fit the "out of sight, out of mind" concept.

As these rolling carts are obviously portable and light, they can be moved easily when the kids want to change the look of their room. They are also smaller than a regular chest of drawers and will fit more easily into closets. Now let's go on and see what we can do for the pre-teen and teen years.

Teens & Clothing

If you have pre-teens or young teens that don't want their clothing in drawers or bins, try the following:

- let them simply fold their clothes and lay them on the closet shelf above the clothes rod (if they're tall enough);

- on special closet shelves that line the closet available at hardware stores;

- on bookcase shelves that you put in the closet;

- on folding tables inside the closet;

- or on permanently installed customized closet shelves.

I keep saying, "in the closet," because it's best not to clutter up the room with furniture. The kids are more interested in "play" or "chat" areas than they are in where their clothes are.

Mid-teens eventually like their clothes folded within dresser drawers and their slacks, shirts, dresses and blouses hung on hangers.

Girls seem to be quicker at discovering that wrinkled clothes are a "no-no" among their peers; boys catch on later.

Speaking of where their clothes are, they're usually on the floor, aren't they? Let's talk about possible solutions to this problem.

Using Hooks Rather than Hangers

Kids of all ages like to drop their clothes on the floor – they'll pick them up "later." Teach them early how to hang items up easily by

- installing hooks behind their bedroom door,

- or at the door they usually use when coming into or leaving the house.
- Line the closet walls with hooks and let them hang all their clothes.
- Arrange hooks all around the bedroom at heights convenient to everyone sharing that room.

- These hooks can be big and plastic and come in different colors so that you can assign a certain color to each child.

Don't worry, they'll get the hang of hangers as they get older and want to look nice. With clothes hanging from hooks all around the room you won't have to spend money on decorating! However, if you're really creative, you can create artistic scenes on the walls around these hooks so that the clothes are actually camouflaged!

To save many of the headaches associated with chests of drawers or lack of space, why not try another approach, a made-to-order closet.

Customized Closets

An ideal way to handle clothing, etc. is to have a customized closet that either you build or have a professional build. You can have shelves, baskets, drawers, clothes rods, etc., all the way your kids need it.

Go to stores that sell these closet re-makes so you can get an idea of what'll work for your children. Since you customize this closet the way the kids need it, it'll be easier for them to keep up with de-cluttering their rooms.

- Use roll out wire baskets for clothes (which you can still put the pictures on, or label).

Use drawers for their toys (which can also have pictures or labels attached).

- The clothes rods could be made so that they are at the right height for them now, with the ability to be raised as the kids grow.

- The drawers or wire baskets can have dividers built into them so that socks, underwear, T-shirts, etc. can be folded and arranged in an upright position so that retrieval is a snap.

- Or the drawers can be used for out-of-season storage, while the wire baskets are used for the current season. The plastic drawers will keep dust off of these stored items.

- Shelves can be built in that hold books, stuffed animals, large toys (dolls, trucks), shoes, etc.

All of these things help to hold the clutter at bay, except possibly for laundry, so let's talk about that when kids share a room and laundry piles up.

Sharing Rooms

When you have two or more children sharing a room, they usually set up territorial boundaries. Even adults like their own space, so how can we blame children for wanting space as well. Try some of the following options to help you maintain your sanity while they're maintaining their space. Let's start with their clothes.

Laundry Options

Finding kids clothes all over the Floor? **Clutter Start!!** Well, don't despair. Let's try a few things to remove this sight.

- Buy an over-the-door basketball laundry hoop. This is available from variety stores or catalog companies. You put a laundry hamper or basket beneath the hoop. This will at least challenge the kids to toss their clothes into the hoop, for awhile anyway.

- Provide three baskets of different colors so that they are encouraged to learn how to separate their clothes into whites, light colors and dark colors. If they are very young, the different colors will be educational (like the cubbies). When they are older they may even be able to get to college and not come home with all pink clothing!

- If you don't like the open baskets, give the kids a container (like a small trash can usually seen in kitchens) for laundry that has a foot pedal so they don't have to think about picking up a lid or replacing it. These containers are fairly small, so get at least three, hopefully in different colors, so they can separate the clothing into the whites, lights and colors. If you can't find any in different colors, mark the cans so they know where to put their clothes.

- Another option is to use different colored mesh bags for each child's laundry that you can hang on a closet wall or behind a door. These bags are available from variety stores and catalog companies.

With more than one child needing laundry help, you will have to decide whether each child needs his or her own "laundry center" or they can all use one system, hopefully that of three different baskets, containers, or bags.

With some training and coaching they will start to recognize that when the bags get full and they have no clothes in their drawers, it's time to do the laundry. A child of ten is capable of doing laundry, so start training them early. When the laundry is done, it needs a "home" to go to, but where?

Assigning Drawers

Assign specific dresser drawers for each child. If you have two children and four drawers, this is easy. Give the shorter child the lower drawers. If you have three children and four drawers, have the three share the extra drawer, but be careful.

If you have them put their underwear in a shared drawer, they'll be fighting over socks. Instead, in that one drawer, have one child put T-shirts; the second child slacks; and the third child, underwear. That way when the drawer gets messy, the fights won't be over who stole whose socks, but who's going to fix the mess. And guess what? Since each child has their own bin, they are responsible for their own mess. Get three plastic bins for the drawer so that the three have their own "space."

You can also put their names on the drawers, or pictures, so that each one knows what's in the drawers and whose drawer (or section) it is. This is particularly helpful for the child who has ADD or dyslexia. Another help for these children is the use of color.

Colorizing

You could try "colorizing" your small children so that they will always know whose clothing belongs to whom. One child wears only blue and red, another wears only pink and purple, a third wears only brown and white. How adventurous are you? Or are they? Yet another solution to keep some peace is to divide the closets.

Dividing Closets

Divide closet areas evenly for the number of children sharing the closet.

- Paint each section different colors,

- Or, hang a sheet or blanket from a hanger from the clothes rod that shows where one section stops and another one starts.

- To make it easier on the children, take the closet doors off and store them on the rafters in the garage, or lay them along the back wall of the closet and brace them so they don't fall down. It really doesn't matter what the closet itself looks like if the kids can't get to what they want **Now**. Remember the saying, "I want what I want when I want it?" If you have closet doors that have to slide past each other, it's really difficult to get to the middle of the closet for anything, and for kids, it's a nightmare. I'm willing to state that many closet doors are off-track as we speak!

If you have a lot of room, the doors could be put on top of 2 two-drawer file cabinets and used as a desk or some other needed counter space. This only works, however, if the doors are flat and not made out of thin metal.

Each child has unique needs. Let them hang, fold or "bin" whatever they wish. You take a holiday! If it's organized their way, they will tend to put things away where they belong and where they can find them. And if you've made it easier for them to retrieve items by using pictures or labels, their lives will be less complicated. Well, let's move out of the closet and talk about how to dress beds!

Bed Making

Don't you just see red when you walk into your child's room and the bed still isn't made? Especially when you've told her at least twenty times to make the bed? Well, have you ever really watched her try to make that bed? She can barely coordinate her dainty little fingers around crayons to draw within the lines, and YOU want her to negotiate the bottom sheet, the top sheet, the blanket, the bedspread and the pillow! Come on, give the little cutie a break!

- Try using water bed sheets on the beds since the top and bottom sheets are sewn together at the bottom. The top sheet can be literally pulled towards the head of the bed without the bottom of the sheet coming loose.

- Or sew the top and bottom sheets together yourself for the same effect. Pin the blanket underneath the mattress so it can also be pulled and straightened without a lot of fuss.

- Use comforters for bedspreads, since bedspreads are really difficult to arrange. You have to be very dedicated to get it just right. Now, I know your child is brilliant, but this is not the place to have him prove it. I gave up on bedspreads years ago when I discovered how easy comforters are.

- For a twin bed, buy a double bed size comforter, for a double, buy a queen, etc. You can then pin the excess portion of the comforter under the mattress, again making it easier for the kids to make.

- During the summer, use an extra top sheet as the "bedspread." Match it to the overall theme of the room. (Be sure to attach it to the underneath of the mattress.) If you put the bed against a wall, pinning the excess on the wall side makes for a neater looking bed.

- If you like to have a pillow sham on the pillow to match the comforter so the bed looks "fancy," just let her place the pillow on the bed and lay the sham on top of the pillow. You probably will have to straighten it out, but hey, she made the bed!

We've walked through the ages of our children by looking at the baby's room to the teen's room, what their closets can do and even options in choosing what to wear. Now let's talk about those other items that drive every one of us to distraction, starting with the toys.

Playthings

"Mooommm, I'm boorrred. I've got nuthin' to do!" So whined my four grandchildren one day. Ever notice how quickly children get bored with a roomful of toys? My daughter solved this problem and here's the trick: Get seven boxes with lids (plastic or cardboard) and mark each one with a day of the week, Sunday through Saturday. Then have each child gather all their toys together. If they are old enough, let them pick out toys they would like to play with for each day of the week. For instance, if they have 35 toys, then help them choose five toys for Sunday, five for Monday, and so on. One box per day for all the children should work. If the toys are really large, you will have to put them in a locked cabinet or closet that they can't get into.

Let's say that today is Wednesday. You take down the box marked "Wednesday" and the kids get to play only with the toys that are in today's box. At the end of the day, all the toys are put back into the box (by the kids) and the box is placed on a closet shelf or other high space that the kids can't get to. Tomorrow you take down Thursday's box and they play with that box's toys only, and so on.

When it rains or snows and the kids are under foot all day, rotate the boxes throughout the day. Let them play with one box for one to one-and-a-half hours and then have them put those toys away and start playing with the next box. Variety is the spice of life! Now, where are your toys?

Need other rainy day ideas? Let's go!

Rainy Day Play

- Have craft projects ready to work on, but only rainy day ones.
- Help the kids build forts out of blankets throughout the house.
- Draw faces on the window panes with your fingers, and have the kids copy.

- Hold contests for the neatest drawers, or fastest clean up of toys after the one hour play session (give treats of ice cream or something special they enjoy).

- Let the kids be messy on rainy days, or days that they cant get out doors. It makes it easier for them to be stuck indoors all day.

- Put on special music, or videos.

- Take the kids to a museum, or the mall, or visit relatives or friends.

- Have a party with another Mom. Trade off party days – goodies are whatever either of you can find in the house, or whatever the kids can make.

- Have a cooking class with your kids.

Puzzles

If you and your children really like to work with puzzles, you know how frustrating it can get when someone knocks a box on the floor, or bumps into the table the puzzle is on. What can really make you pull your hair out is when all the puzzle boxes are knocked on the floor and you have hundreds of puzzle pieces everywhere.

To avoid puzzle mix-ups, take each puzzle and mark the backside of each piece with some letter, number or symbol that lets you know which puzzle that piece belongs to. Some of my clients put their puzzle pieces into zip-lock bags and throw the box away because it takes up too much room. They cut the picture off the box so that they have something to look at while trying to get the puzzle solved.

Collections

Like the old woman in the shoe, does your child have so many stuffed toys, hats and such that you don't know what to do?

Consider some usual, and not so usual suggestions and recommendations.

Bill caps can be corralled on wall hat holders that are now shown in catalogs and variety stores. There are floor-to-ceiling tension poles that have clips to hold caps. You can also hang them from pegs attached to wall holders, stack them one atop another on a closet shelf or in a dresser drawer, or hang them from hooks all around the room. If these caps are not used, nail them to the walls near the ceiling. If they are being kept as collectibles, put them in a plastic bin with a snap-lock lid. You can keep the bugs out by putting a few cedar chips in the bin. Avoid moth balls. Ugh! You'll never get the smell out.

The stuffed toys can be settled into a net that hangs in a corner and is attached to each wall so that it resembles a hammock. They can also be hung from a floor-to-ceiling tension pole, or hung from chain clips. Or set them on shelves that line the walls, or from pegs or hooks that line the walls. And if you're really clever, you can nail them to the walls near the ceiling so that the toys look like they're free floating! Like the caps, if some of these toys are collectibles, put them in a storage bin.

Wherever the collection is in the room, your child will need to keep them clean and dust free. Yes, that is part of the process of letting them keep their possessions. They must learn that collecting isn't just keeping what they want, it also entails tending to them and caring for them.

When the collections get to be really too big and generally unused or unappreciated, it is then that you should try to convince your child that they have too many bunnies, hats, and other toys. Ask them if they think they are old enough to give up some of these things by giving them to a little boy or girl who doesn't have any.

My clients are much more willing to give away their things if they are going to someone who needs them, for example, a woman's shelter, rather than the trash bin, or even to the usual collection places. Donate these clean used toys to day care centers, pre-schools or doctor's offices.

School Things

Let's turn our attention now to what happens when our children go to school.

Schedules

When children start back to school in the fall, one of the first pieces of paper to get lost is the class schedule. If this isn't already typed up for them, try to have it typed and then laminate it. Office supply stores usually offer this service. If you can color code their schedules for them with highlighters, that would be even better. Once the schedule is laminated, 3-hole punch it and place it at the front of a binder.

Let's look at what can be done about homework.

- Behind the schedule have dividers for each of their classes. Within each divider, have a sheet protector. A divider with pockets is also useful, depending on the need of the student. The pocket dividers come in heavy paper stock, but they also come in plastic, which is what I would recommend, since children are pretty rough with their notebooks.

- When homework is done, instead of the child shoving it in any onvenient opening, they can put it in the sheet protector for the subject they've done homework on. The pocket dividers allow the child to receive things from a class and have a "home" to put it in. When they get home, the sheet protector will be empty because they've turned their homework in, and the pocket dividers will have homework paperwork in them that they've received. On their way to school the next day, the pockets should be empty because the sheet protectors will have their homework in it.

- In the front of the notebook, just in front of their schedule, a useful item is a zippered pocket in which they can carry their pencils, pens, markers, rulers and calculators. Let them also carry post-it notes so that they can mark something in their book that they need to pay attention to. Like doing their homework!

Homework

He lost his homework again. I am sure that every teacher out there wishes she had a nickel for every child who lost homework. The problem is, many of these kids actually did lose their homework.

After talking to my young clients, their problems with paper are about the same as for adults. It doesn't matter that homework is important and needs to be turned in. Bills are important to be paid, but they get "lost" too! Children seem to be carrying more and more books to school and with no overnight lockers available are forced to carry huge backpacks on their tiny little bodies. It's no wonder they can't find their paperwork.

Along with schedules and homework, there is also paperwork that ends up everywhere. Let's look at some options for these papers.

Activity Binders

Children bring reams of paper home every day (a slight exaggeration, but that's how I felt when my kids came home from school). To handle these papers, try the following:

- Set up a 3-ring activity binder for each child. Use index tab dividers and show them how to keep their papers separated by different subjects.

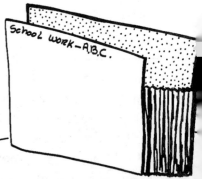

You can also get expandable pocket files that either fit in a drawer or on a shelf. They are like a file folder but are closed on both sides, and expand from 3 to 5 inches depending on the type you buy. They also come in a hanging file style to use in a file cabinet. You or your child can walk around with them without having papers falling to the floor (**Clutter Start!**).

Keep these papers only if they want to keep them. At the end of the school year, have your child look at what they kept, decide what they still want to keep, and then have them throw out the rest (not you!).

In my work with adults, whose problems are generally saving and hoarding everything, I have found they often have something in common that goes back to their childhood. Their mother, father, both, or another caregiver, made the decision whether papers, or other toys/possessions would stay or go.

Try to think back to when you were a child, sitting on the floor happily playing with a toy that you love. An adult walks in and declares that you're too old to play with that toy, or that the toy is too old, too worn out, or too dirty and – poof – the toy is gone. So now these adults, all grown up, hang on to everything they have, just to show that they can. Please do not do this to your children.

But what about all those art projects that they so lovingly insist that you display with pride?

Children's Art

Children are very proud of their artwork and they love to see it displayed. We usually display these cherished pieces on the refrigerator and then before we know it, we can't see the refrigerator!

To help you find your refrigerator again, and to help the kids learn to make choices, display their art for up to two weeks only. At the end of one or two weeks, have them pick the two best pieces (one per week) and put these into a 3-ring binder within sheet protectors, in a file folder or keepsake box, inside a picture frame, or on a corkboard.

This means that the other artwork gets thrown away. Be sure that it is the child that does this and not you. This will get them used to the idea that even paper has a life time to it – a birth, growth, maturity and death.

After one month (mark it on a calendar), keep the best one of the four. Keeping one piece per month will give you twelve pieces per year. This will be easier to save than dozens of artwork pieces. Possibly at the end of the year you can convince them to keep one great picture from the whole year!

If they insist on keeping everything, then you have to get a little dramatic. If you are keeping these items in a binder, let them keep all that can possibly get into the binder. Once it is full, all you need to say is, "Gee, the binder's full. What are we going to do?" (This is the one reason why I recommend binders over any other method.) Buying another binder is out of the question. They have to eventually get around to making decisions about what to keep and what to get rid of.

An "out" for you (if they really get hysterical over throwing things away) might be to tell them they can have another binder on their birthday and that you will buy a binder for each year of their life at home, until they are old enough to say to stop, or until they are 18, whichever comes first.

Their rooms must be able to store these binders on bookshelves or closet shelves. Do not stack them into the communal living areas (living room, dining room, family room, kitchen, bathrooms, hallways, laundry rooms). Keep only what they want to keep, rather than what you want to keep. If you want to keep it, put it in with your keepsakes, not theirs. Storage boxes can hold these binders.

Storage Boxes

Just like us, kids feel a need to connect with their past and belong. Their possessions (toys, mementos, awards, etc.) give them this good sense of self. When their binders get full and they've collected awards for various achievements, they need a "permanent" home for them. Storage boxes fill this need.

- Buy plastic ten to twelve gallon storage bins with snap-lock lids. Make them big enough to store many items, yet small enough to be manageable if stored on shelves in the garage or on the top shelves of closets.

- Ask your children if they would like to decorate this box, especially if the box will be staying in their room. You can use contact paper, tempura paints, or even some of the artwork that once lived on the refrigerator. An older child would be more inclined to do this than a three year old, so the storage box may have to stay free of adornment until your child shows some interest in scribbling on it. The teenager may look at their once lovingly adorned box and laugh, but they probably won't throw it away until they become an adult. And then again they may keep it to show it to their children.

Time for Mom and Dad

Now that we've got the kids all settled with their rooms, their clothes and their schoolwork, what about you? Had any time off lately? Are you laughing at me? Read on!

Babysitting

OK you two. It's time for both of you to get out of the house and enjoy yourselves. But what do you do with the children? In former times, when many families lived close to each other, children were left with relatives who would babysit. Today, so many people live far from relatives and don't like the idea of using day care centers. In checking with my clients, some of their babysitting resources have come from the following:

- High school work programs
- Sitting services
- Babysitting cooperatives
- Houses of worship
- Senior centers

The high school program and the Senior center worked out the best for them. This may or may not be the same in your local area. Interviews had been set up to talk to the referrals so that they were comfortable leaving the children when they were able to have a night out.

If any of you have come up with other great ideas, please write to me at CLUTTER STOP®, PO Box 2014, Upland CA 91785-2014. I will be sure to mention it in my next book!

Well, we've wound our way through most of the rooms in your house. I hope you're feeling less stressed over your clutter and have some clear ideas on how to proceed when you decide to stop the clutter – if you didn't do it as we went room by room!

Summary

- Signs of low self-esteem is a painfully obvious one – clutter.
- All children benefit from a healthy dose of self-esteem.
- If children with ADD/LD learn to conquer their home environment, this strength can then bolster them in the external environment.
- The first essential item in a child's room is the bed. Additional con siderations are a changing table and a rocker.
- Excess toys from well-meaning relatives can be stored easily until the child is old enough for them.
- If baby is sharing the room with another child, then dividing the closet now is better than waiting for later when the arguments start.

- Children tend to be floor sleepers or bed sleepers. Create a wonderful and peaceful room for them by whatever they prefer.
- Desks and bookcases are needed as your child grows.
- Teach your children sound choices regarding their clothing options.
- Look at optional storage solutions for shoes, socks, ribbons, etc.
- Teach your children how to share a dresser and how to decide on whether to hang, fold, or "hook' their clothes.
- Sharing rooms can be made easier by assigning drawers, colorizing, and dividing closets.
- Make bed making easier by using less formal bedding.
- Playthings – use 7 boxes for each day of the week to keep your children from being bored.
- Be prepared for rainy day play with games, crafts or outings
- Label the underside of puzzles so accidental droppings don't drive you mad.
- Gently coax your children into streamlining their collections.
- Tackle the homework and school problems quickly by setting up a working binder that your child can easily use.
- Teach your children how to care for their artwork and other precious papers by having storage boxes just for them.
- Don't forget about yourself, Mom and Dad. Look into the various babysitting options available in your city.

I Will:

- create an open and warm place to where my child can retreat;
- teach my child how to care for their belongings;
- teach my child the importance of keeping the best of what they do and letting go of just everyday paperwork;
- teach my child how to curb hoarding by showing them how to make choices;
- teach my child how to share their space with others;
- teach my child that items must be returned to their homes;
- help my child grow up with as many tools and tips as I can find;
- congratulate myself on a job well done!!

Our last stop before leaving your home is to now attack all those papers hanging around. Just sit down and relax. It isn't all that bad! You can basically just sit, decide, put away or throw away. If you have a "wheelie chair," it's even easier!

After all, according to Walter Elliott, "Perseverance is not a long race; it is many short races one after another." Amen! I will not desert you, I am right here. Tomorrow we'll start your papers!

CHAPTER NINE

Putrid Paper Predicament

Oh, That Paper!

Every day they come marching in, without any regard for your feelings! They don't care if you're sick, overwhelmed, or just plain tired. And yet you know that you have to deal with them. No, not your children, your putrid papers! They do stink when we don't know what to do with them all.

How do you deal with paper clutter, especially that generated by incoming mail? Come sit beside me as I explain. It isn't difficult, but it does require time, but not an **All Day Marathon!** This is definitely an area where I want you to take your time and make careful decisions.

Typical Evening Scene

Let's first take a look at a typical evening scene. You just got home from work and brought the mail into the house. You tear open the envelopes, letting them flutter to the floor. You briefly look at the contents, your eyes glaze over, and then you just toss the papers on the kitchen counter, desk, couch, chair, dining room table, floor or anything else that has a flat surface. And you know that the floor is not an option!

You don't have time to look at the mail because you must fix dinner, or take the kids to soccer, or go to Bible study, or get your hair cut, or work on the boss' report, or your favorite team is playing tonight. By the time you get back to looking at the mail you're too tired to care and just let it lie in a heap or add it to the growing pile on your desk. You've just started the **Clutter Start!** process, or you're continuing it.

And you think to yourself, "Why am I such a slob when MaryJane down the street has as many kids as I do and she's so organized?" You don't know that she's organized, but that's what you see when you walk into her home. You have no idea what's hiding in drawers or closets.

Opening mail and making decisions on what to do with the mail is so stressful that some people just "freak out." Some of my clients with Attention Deficit Disorder (ADD) just sit down and almost cry when they try to figure out what to do with it all. They absolutely lose control, and control is what they need the most. As a friend of mine recently said, who has ADD, "I just get so Dis-Trackted." She isn't the only one. Many of us get off-track! But, I'm going to get you back on the right track!

Why Papers Are Important

So that you understand why paper processing is important, let me explain. Every home, whether it consists of one person or ten, is a business. And every business has to deal with money and papers. Look at the following points:

- You have money coming in – typically from paychecks, rents, interest or dividends. Businesses call this money accounts receivable.

- You also have money going out – typically in credit card purchases, groceries, or checks for utilities and other bills. Businesses call this money accounts payable.

- You have allowances you pay to yourself and your children. Businesses call this money salaries.

- You have big ticket item expenses – like cars, refrigerators, washer/ dryers, and furniture. Businesses call big ticket items capital expenditures.

- You have personal medical/dental/vision premiums you have to pay and gift items you purchase to keep your spouse and children happy. You also have vacation/sick leave/personal days, which you do have to plan for if you need child/animal care while you're away or ill. Businesses call all these items their benefit package.

So, you see, you do run a business. In order to run your home "business," files will need to be set up to keep your business running smoothly. And no, we won't be setting up accounting files, but we will be setting up files run on the same accounting principles just discussed. I'll go through the types of files you want to keep and how to set them up, and also show you different methods to handle your incoming mail.

Get Ready, Get Set

To head off that hopeless despair when you daily see more paper coming into your home, you need to choose a place to do battle with that pile of paper, to knock it down to size. We're going to talk about the best place for you to put your papers, the supplies you'll need and then a step-by-step process to help you through the putrid paper predicament!

However, if you've never set up files before and basically haven't a clue where to start, then let me address you as "Q" because you're questioning whether you can do this. Continue reading, but watch for the "Q" address.

The Best Place

On a daily basis, until you're prepared to wage the paper battle, leave all the mail in a chosen place and always in that same place every day. In that place you will need two holding containers, one for the bills and one for the rest of the incoming papers. These containers can be baskets or trays that are dedicated to the unsorted, incoming mail or other papers that come into the house from shopping, church, or other sources. The chosen place to put these containers can be a small table in your foyer, a drawer in the kitchen, on a desk, or on the end table in your family room right next to your favorite chair!

Try not to put any other papers or items into this holding area. It's not meant to be a catchall. It's for the special purpose of holding your mail until you can attack it.

It's important for you to have two different containers so that your bills don't get lost among the other mail.

After we're done with your general papers and where to file them, I will also show you how to set up your Tax Files. Check with your tax person for information on the length of time to keep certain papers.

Before you start doing anything, however, please read through this entire chapter. Some of this information may be "old news" for some of you, while others of you have never heard the word "hanging File" before (my Q people!).

When you're ready to open the mail and/or pay bills, take the mail from its container to where you plan on opening and processing it. But first, in order to process this mail, you will need some "tools."

Necessary Supplies

A letter opener, scissors, pencil and pen, tape, paper clips, stapler, post-it notes and rubber bands need to be right there in a container or drawer to help you open, discard, clip together, make notes on, and so forth, as you process through each piece of paper. A circular file (you know, a waste-basket) should be in the immediate area. A shredder would be another useful tool to have.

Along with the office supplies, you might want to have your calendar, date book or planner and four file folders for sorting. These file folders will hold papers that you receive which need to be filed in your business, household, information or personal categories. These categories will be discussed later in this chapter.

Before you file any papers (yes, I'm going to show you how), you'll need some other office supplies - a file cabinet, file folders, hanging files and labels. Let me discuss these with you before we actually proceed. I will also discuss color coding your files.

Sorry, but this is dry and boring stuff to read. Unfortunately, it's necessary in order for you to understand - finally - how to sort, categorize, label and file all your paper.

File Cabinets

Every home needs a filing cabinet of some sort. It can be a vertical 2-drawer, a horizontal 2-drawer (called a lateral file), a vertical 4-drawer, or a portable filing case. The capacity you need for filing depends on how active your home is.

This file cabinet can possibly be treated as furniture. If it's small, it could be the right size to use as an end table (by placing a nice cover on it). Larger file cabinets require their own space and are probably not useful as a furniture piece.

File Folders

You'll also need file folders and/or hanging files into which your papers will be stored. But before you rush out to buy these files, please read through this chapter. You may want these file folders in different colors for the different categories into which you'll divide your papers.

When you buy your file folders, in order to make a more informed decision, the following information on the different types of file folders is offered; most file folders are called "manila" file folders. They come in either letter size (9 1/2" H x 11 3/4" W) or legal size (9 1/2" H x 14 3/4" W).

- Straight cut file folders. These folders have one tab that runs across the entire top of the file. These can be used for multiple labels or when labels are extra long or if you want all of your file folders to l look exactly the same. You may have to special order these from your office supply store.

- Half-cut file folders. These folders have tabs across the top that covers one half of the file folder, with some cut to the left and the rest cut to the right. They are used for long headings, or if you want certain files all to the left with the rest all to the right. You may have to special-order these also.

- One-third cut file folders. These are the file folders typically sold in office supply stores. One-third cut means that three tab positions are on the top. Some of the tabs are cut to the top left, some are on the top middle, and some are on the top right. In alphabetical filing, if you use all three positions starting from the left, the staggered positions of the tabs make it easier to see A, B, and C files because one tab isn't hiding another.

- One-fifth cut file folders. These files have five tab positions across the top. These tabs are very narrow and are staggered cut so that if you place each different cut tab behind the other, starting at the left, you would be able to see all five tabs. These file folders are mostly used for numerical filing systems. They are a special order item also.

- There are also end tab file folders - typically used in medical offices - which also come in straight cut or l/3 cut. Somewhat like the l/3 cut tabs on regular file folders, there are three tab positions, but they are on the shorter 9 1/2" W side, with a tab at the top, middle or bottom of the file folder. They typically stick out from a shelf and are not used in file cabinets. These file folders may be what you want if you're putting your sheet music on shelves or in bookcases.

There are also "interior" file folders that are 9 inches high, including the tab and do not show above the hanging file, hence the name "interior." It will be your personal choice as to which type of file folders you want to use. Interior file folders cost more than regular file folders and are only available in the l/3 cut positions.

Or, try looking at other filing systems to see if you like one method better than another (I personally use regular l/3 cut file folders so that I can see each one when I open the file cabinet. I don't like interior file folders because it means that I have to search inside of a hanging file to find the file I want. But, those are my files!). Interior file folders, however, make for a very neat looking file drawer.

Another option: some of my clients use only the hanging files without file folders. It's up to you. These are your files!

You might want to experiment with which type of file folders suit you better before you spend money on one kind only to discover that you really hate it. Start with just one topic – say, Business files, and buy just enough folders for that topic in whatever color or style of file folder that you like. This will keep your expense down and will help you decide what you really want. And don't let anyone talk you into what you need. You must be able to find the paperwork you're looking for after it's filed and that will only happen when it's your system.

Q: Always use a hanging file with file folders. Buy the hanging file and folders typically sold at the stores – olive green hanging files and manila file folders in l/3 cut. But read on, and I will list more things for you to do so that you don't have to decide what to do. When you get comfortable with your filing system, then you can start making your own decisions. So fear not!

Hanging Files

Hanging files are heavy file folders that have little metal hooks that stick out from each end of the hanging file. These hooks rest on rods that sit at the inside tops of the file drawer. Some file cabinets are made so that these hooks can rest on the top edges of the drawer. Hanging files are used to hold several related file folders, i.e., medical records on your family.

If you have too much paper in the file folders within your hanging file and they are not sitting well enough to close your drawer, add another file folder and/or an additional hanging file behind the first one. You won't necessarily need to label this additional hanging file because it's just behind the first one. However, if you find this unnerving, you can label the first hanging file as #1 and the second one as #2 (as in Medical #1 and Medical #2). Don't forget to label your file folder. I will give you more information on labeling and filing later in this chapter.

When there are many papers that belong to one file, such as in the Medical #1 and #2 above, you can also use hanging files known as "box bottom" hanging files. They allow more folders to be in one hanging file if you like all your folders together in one file. Note: the box bottom hanging files cost more than regular hanging files and expand from one inch to five inches.

Q: I don't want you to file more papers just because you have the room, so for right now please buy the regular hanging files and use two or more if you need more space.

Labeling File Folders

It doesn't matter what you choose to call your files, as long as the names are familiar and understandable to you. (For example, Medical can be labeled Health, Doctor, My Body, etc.)

- You can label your files with pen or marker right on the file tab itself. In order to read the label, try to print very large and use a dark color.

Q: Buy a black felt marker to label all your files. If you have a label maker, use it. If you have a computer program for labels, use it.

- You can also print on a file label that you stick on the tab. These can be purchased separately and come in all white, or white with a colored top border. The colored border may be helpful to you if you're trying to color coordinate certain files.

- You can also type on the labels, use a label machine or use a computer program for labels.

Labeling Hanging Files

Hanging files come with removable clear plastic tabs with white paper-board inserts. You can hand print these tabs, use a label maker or a computer program. The standard color of these files is olive green.

Q: Just like you did for your file folder labels, use a black felt pen, your label maker, or your computer program on these inserts.

- Once you've labeled the insert, put it into the plastic tab. Then place the tab into the slots located inside the hanging file at the top. Where you place the tab is up to you. There are slots across the entire top of the folder, both front and back. You can stagger them to the left, middle and right, or place them in the same position for each hanging file you use. Again, this is personal preference and how it affects you when you open the file cabinet. Some people like the tab in the front of the hanging file, while others prefer it in the back. I put mine in front as it's easier to see because my files stick up above the hanging files (remember, I'm not using interior file folders).

Q: For now, put all your plastic tabs on the front side of the hanging file and place them all to the left.

- I recommend that you buy the longer size plastic tabs (1/3 cut). A regular standard size comes with the letter size hanging files, but they are shorter, making it difficult to print big or label with a longer heading. The 1/3 tabs also come in color, but you may have to special-order them.

Color Coding

Some people like to color code their files. This can either excite you, or drive you crazy. It's exciting because you can go directly to a specific color in your filing cabinet and know immediately where to start looking.

On the other hand, when you need to file something new, you must have that particular color file folder on hand, and possibly a hanging file and plastic tab as well.

- The standard file folder colors that stores carry are blue, green, red and yellow. Some stores may also carry purple. Other colors can be special ordered.

- Hanging files also come in colors. The usual colors are blue, green, red and yellow. Some stores may carry purple. Other colors can be special ordered.

Now that we've discussed the supplies you need, let's talk about what to do with those boxes of paper I had you stack against the wall when we first started working. In order to do this we must divide the work in order to conquer the problem.

Divide and Conquer!

To divide and conquer the problem I will start by walking you though four steps to get control over these papers:

1. Sorting into Four Types of Files,

2. Deciding on Categories,

3. Setting up Files, and

4. Illustrating what goes in the files.

Please read this entire paper chapter so that you can get the whole picture on how to proceed before you compulsively try to perfect it!

Four distinct types of papers come into your home:

- Business (financial items),

- Household (everything regarding your home),

- Information and/or Resources (future purchases, activities, information),

- Personal (all about you, your family and friends).

These are the four general types of papers that we'll divide all your papers into. The best way to gain control over papers is to sort them, then file them. When we're through sorting, we'll have four piles of papers - business, household, information and personal. These are just four types of papers, not specific categories. We will then divide these papers, and then divide again, and divide them again, and ... let's just start!

Grab four boxes and label them: business, household, information, and personal. If you sorted the papers when we first started through your home, great, otherwise you'll need to gather all the boxes of paper you've collected so we can start sorting.

Four Types of Papers

The first type of papers to look for are all your "Business" papers. These are all the papers having to do with current money matters. Some general examples of these records are:

- Car Payment Receipts/Repair Receipts
- Credit Card Receipts
- Investments
- Medical Receipts (not medical history information)
- Mortgage or Rental Receipts
- Rental Property Receipts
- Tax Records
- Utility Receipts

The second type of papers that we need to find are "Household" papers, a collection of papers on things that are generally associated with your home. Some general examples are:

- Home Services
- Household Appliances
- Household Improvements (if you own a home)
- Purchases
- Warranty Booklets/Instructions

The third type of papers to gather up are the "Information" or "Resource" type of papers. Some general examples are:

- Directions
- Personal Services

- Restaurants
- Things to Buy
- Trips (Day, Overseas, Vacation, Weekend)

The fourth type of papers that we need to deal with are all your "Personal" papers about you and your family. Some general examples are:

- Employment contracts/resumes
- Family members correspondence
- Friends correspondence
- Health records (Medical, Dental, Vision, Chiropractic, etc.)
- Hobbies
- Memorabilia
- Military records
- Passports (these would be safer in a safe deposit box)
- Religious activities
- School records
- Volunteering

These four areas constitute the majority of all papers that you would want to keep and organize so you can find them easily. So our first task is to do a general sort into these four types of papers. Right now these papers are still in the boxes that we collected while going through your home. And remember, there is another secret file: the wastebasket!

AND HERE'S A WORD ABOUT THE LOWLY WASTEBASKET

Any papers you have that contain sensitive information, such as your social security number, credit card numbers, or any account number would be best torn up before they are discarded. Better yet, invest in a paper shredder, an item available in all business supply stores and even discount stores at a very reasonable price. Shredding sensitive documents foils any attempt made by someone trying to steal your identity, which is a current and growing problem.

Creating Your Filing System

Now that we are separating your papers into the four general types of files, we need to throw away unnecessary papers (outdated coupons, last year's concert tickets, etc.). This may be an area that is difficult for you, so as you're sorting ask yourself some questions on the items you're not sure about:

- Is this information current?
- Do I still have this product that this warranty book is for?
- Is this a memorabilia item that can be put into a memory box?
- Can I get this information on the internet or at the public library if I need it?
- Is this my current utility bill, or an old paid bill?

   If your current bill shows that last month's bill was paid, you can shred or discard last month's bill. If you need it for proof of residency, you can get copies from the utility company. Why clutter up your files?

- Is this my current credit card statement?

   If yes, and it shows you paid last month's bill, you can throw last month's away. If you feel there might be a dispute over a purchase, then keep the statements in question. Don't be afraid to shred or throw these away, either. If you're really fearful, keep the last three statements only or contact your accountant for further advice.

- Ask yourself: If I file this piece of paper, will I ever look for it again?

   Keeping papers because that's what everyone else does isn't healthy for you. Every time you open the file drawer you're going to see a sea of paper that you may never need again. Think about this carefully as you finish reading this chapter.

Once the above questions have been answered, you'll be able to carry your sorted papers to your file cabinet when you're ready to file and know exactly where to put them.

I will help you decide on subcategories in each area so that the papers are easier to find. (Don't freak out, just keep reading! And smile!)

Future Look – An organized dream (not a fantasy!)

They look so nice! All your business files are in green, household files are in yellow, information is in red and your personal information is in blue. No more guessing!

Try not to think of this filing system as a permanent place, but as a living and moving thing. There's a birth, a maturing, and then a "death" of all papers. I don't mean that to sound scary or morbid, but, in other words, what you create here should be made up of currently useful papers.

For example, you buy an appliance (birth) and you file the booklet, warranty and sales slip. You then have the appliance repaired (maturing) and you file the repair slip. When you discard the appliance (death), you also discard the warranty/instruction book, the repair slips and the sales slip.

The same goes for your files of bill receipts and so forth. When you receive a utility bill, look to see if it states that they received last month's payment. If they did, then you can throw last month's receipt away. This helps you to be careful so that you don't start a forever collection of papers that are now neatly organized into file cabinets. If you have rental properties, then please check with your accountant or lawyer about the types of papers that you need to keep. Every state has its own regulations.

Penelope

When I first met this woman she had six 4-drawer file cabinets crowding her bedroom, all of which were very organized but were crammed with outdated, useless papers and information. She had collected these papers over 20 years and thought that she had to keep them all. Every utility bill, credit card statement, church program, Christmas card, etc., were all sleeping very comfortably in all her file drawers. She confessed that she never looked for anything in the files – she just filed!

Let's not let your household papers become a life-long collection process. We'll need to keep your papers current by discarding outdated ones, perhaps once or twice a year. If you have tons of old paperwork hanging around, try to find current papers that are no more than three years old to start the process. When we've filed your current paperwork we can then go back and see if there's anything really important in the old papers. Otherwise you might spend years trying to file!

Let me back up a little here and talk about your filing cabinet a moment. I recommend that you separate the four types of files into different file drawers. Separating files into specific drawers will help you to remember where you need to file, or find, your paperwork. For instance, in a 4-drawer vertical cabinet you could put your business section in the top drawer, the household section in the second drawer, information can go in the third drawer, and personal papers can go into the bottom drawer.

If you have a 2-drawer vertical file cabinet, business and household papers can occupy the top drawer and personal and information can share the bottom drawer, depending on how much paperwork you have for each. Also, if you have a 2-drawer lateral file cabinet, it's like having a 4-drawer cabinet. In this type of cabinet you could also put business and household in one drawer and personal and information in the other. If you're using a 2-drawer vertical file cabinet and you find that you need more space, two 2-drawer cabinets would be quite adequate for most family needs.

If you don't already have file cabinets, then you'll have to decide what type to get. Please avoid getting the 18" 2-drawer file cabinets. They just don't give you enough room and the drawers don't open all the way.

Q: Buy a 22" to 26" 2 or 4-drawer file cabinet and be sure that the cabinet drawers pull out all the way.

Filing by Color

I have found that my clients who have Attention Deficit Disorder (ADD), color is a great boost to finding papers. Colored file folders are easier to distinguish in a file cabinet, or if they're left lying somewhere. They can even be memory joggers. But try to keep your color choices to no more than four, otherwise the colors will confuse rather than help.

Also think about whether different colors would be of help to you. Hanging files typically come in a dark olive color. You can choose to use these (they're less expensive) rather than the colored ones and just buy colored file folders to match your categories.

You can also just use the olive hanging files with manila file folders and clear tabs. Or, as most of my clients do to save money, they use the olive hanging files, the manila file folders and the longer (1/3 cut) colored tabs for specific categories. I personally prefer using just the colored tabs – it's less expensive and I don't have to constantly worry about whether I have the right colored file folder or hanging files so that I can file.

Q: Use the standard olive hanging files, manila file folders and the longer l/3 cut plastic tabs, in color for the four types of files.

Following are filing examples for the four types of papers we collect. The examples show when to use a hanging file, tabs, and file folders. They also give suggested colors. These examples are from the filing system that was designed for MaryJane, you know - the neighbor you think is so perfect.

MaryJane

MaryJane owns her home, is married to John, and has two children, April and June. MaryJane volunteers for the school PTA, goes to church and takes her kids to their soccer and ballet classes. You might be interested to know that they are in debt, and have many credit cards! They also filed bankruptcy eight years ago! So what you see isn't necessarily what you get!

After each of the main headings listed below I have included, in parentheses, other names for these files that I have seen when working with clients. As you read, start thinking about the paperwork that you deal with and where you might file it. But don't start working yet!

The first example is for Business type papers. MaryJane decided to use green for this category. We therefore will use green hanging files, file folders and plastic tabs:

Business Papers

Banking (hanging file and plastic tab)(Financial Institutions)

Make a file folder for each banking institution you deal with, including Credit Unions. All statements for each banking account go into these files. Keep the statements for at least three years. (You can archive two of the years in a storage box in a closet or garage as long as you can get to them if you need them.)

- ABC Bank, Checking (file folder)
- ABC Bank, Loan (file folder)
- ABC Bank, Savings (file folder)
- City Credit Union (file folder)

Car Information (hanging file and plastic tab)(Auto; Automobile; Engine; Vehicle)

This is a business type file because it doesn't fall into personal or information. Some people prefer to put this file in Household, and you can certainly put it there, also.

These files are examples of what MaryJane used, but you have to find your files, so put it where you think you would naturally go to look for it. If you're not certain, try it here and see how comfortable you are with it.

Q: Put any car information into the hanging file for your car. If you want to change it later, do so.

For MaryJane we divided her car information into separate folders. You may not want to do this. If you only want one file folder for everything, then have just one file folder. These are just examples.

- Ford - Insurance (file folder - if more than one car, use different folders)

  Be sure to keep your current insurance information in the file. The little insurance card belongs in your wallet.

  This file can also be put with all the other insurance papers (mortgage, property, life, disability, etc.). The Insurance hanging file can be kept in Business, or put in the Household category – again, put it where you can find it.

Q: Put your car insurance folder with all the other insurance papers.

- Ford - Purchase Papers (file folder)

  In this file folder is all the information for this specific car.

- Ford - Repairs (file folder)

  This file folder contains all the paperwork for all the repairs to this car. It's good to keep all repair bills on your car to see how often you're having to fix your car and the possible need to replace it.

- Woe To Me (file folder)

  A strange name - but she knows what it is - it's the accident she got into and it was her fault! Keep all records on any accident as you might need it when you sell the car, or for court records, or for medical reimbursements, etc.

Credit Cards (hanging file and plastic tab)(Foolish Spending; In Debt; Plastic; Sucker Bait)

Paid statements go in here, in individual file folders. Keep the statement you just made a payment on. When next month's statement comes and it shows that your payment was received, you can discard last month's statement unless there's a question on a bought item or if needed for tax records.

Your credit card receipt can be kept in an envelope inside the file folder, or in a holding place you use for all your credit card receipts. The receipts can be shredded or torn up once you match the receipt to the charges on the statement. Attach any receipt for new products to the information/warranty and/or service agreement for that product. This information will be discussed later under the "Household" category.

Once you've checked your receipts against the statement, only keep those that haven't appeared on the current statement, are in question, needed for income tax, or needed for proof of purchase. If you run a business from home, purchases you made on your credit card might be tax deductible. Check with your tax person.

- American Express (file folder)(Card that Replaces Broken Items; Prestige Card)
- Discover (file folder) (Card #2)
- Master Card (file folder) (Card #3; Good Everywhere Card; Overseas Card)
- Visa (file folder) (Card #4; Dangerous Limits)

Income (hanging file and plastic tab)

Pay stubs can be filed here until you receive your year-end 1099 or W2 statement from your employer. You can then file these stubs with your tax records, or in an archive file. MaryJane sometimes does part-time work, so we included a file for her also.

- Pay Stubs - John (file folder)
- Pay Stubs - MaryJane (file folder)

Investments (hanging files and plastic tab)

A hanging file that says "Investments" may not be necessary here. If you have many different investments, it might be best to have a hanging file for each type of investment – bonds, house papers, IRA's, mutual funds, rental property, retirement accounts and stocks.

Always keep the original investment information, all additional purchases, sales, and the year-end summaries for all the years you hold the investment. This will be needed for taxes when you sell or cash the funds.

Q: Use a hanging file and different file folders for each investment.

We set MaryJane up with hanging files for each of her investments. (They are still color coordinated green as we are still in business type papers.)

- Bonds (hanging file and plastic tab)
- NBC Bonds (file folder)
- Inner City Bond (file folder)
- 123 Main Street (hanging file and plastic tab)(Our Home)
- Improvements (file folder) (Upgrades; Additions; Construction)
  These are tax deductible items at time of sale.
- Maintenance (file folder)

  This is strictly information on normal maintenance for your home and items that don't usually get deducted at time of sale (painting, for instance). This just gives you a good record of how often you do maintenance and what products you used.
- Mortgage (file folder)

  All the mortgage statements go here, as well as any payment stubs. This file can also go into the Household section of your files, if you prefer. The year-end statement from the Mortgage Company that shows how much interest you've paid will go into your tax files.

IRA Accounts (hanging file and plastic tab)

- CBS IRA Account - MaryJane (file folder)
- SEP IRA Account - John (file folder)
  Mutual Funds (hanging file and plastic tab)
- ABC Mutual Fund (file folder)
- Hearts and Flowers Mutual Fund (file folder)

Rental – 123 Center Street (hanging file and plastic tab)

- Rental Agreement (file folder)
- Rental Earnings (file folder)
- Repairs/Maintenance (file folder)
- Stewart, Jane - Tenant (file folder)

Rental – 123 Wandering Lane (hanging file and plastic tab)

- Rental Agreement (file folder)
- Rental Earnings (file folder)
- Repairs/Maintenance (file folder)
- Thompson, Sue - Tenant (file folder)

Retirement Accounts (hanging file and plastic tab)

- Military Retirement - John (file folder)
- USA University Retirement Funds - MaryJane (file folder)

Stock Accounts (hanging file and plastic tab)

- CBS Stock (file folder)
- Fly By Nite Stock (file folder)

Worst Nightmare (hanging file, file folders and tab)

This is what MaryJane called her bankruptcy file. In here she keeps all the records pertaining to the bankruptcy and how they dealt with it. She keeps it as a reminder to not get into debt again (but we know she has).

Utilities (hanging file and plastic tab)

Use a file folder for each of the following statements – when a new bill comes in, check to be sure that last month's bill is showing as paid, and then discard last month's statement. There is no need to keep past statements unless you need them for income tax reasons (i.e., writing off a home office).

- Electric (file folder)
- Gas (file folder)
- Lawn Service (file folder)
- Pest Control (file folder)
- Pool Service (file folder)

- Security Alarm (file folder)

- Telephone (file folder, or folders if more than one system)

- Water (file folder)

Okay, take a breather! Quit reading or quit working. Time for a break! Sit down for a few minutes or grab a drink and I'll see you back here in about 15 minutes.

Household Papers

Our next category is for "Household" type records. Let's use Yellow hanging files, file folders and tabs. These files are for everything pertaining to your home. (All papers dealing with improvements/upgrades to your home must be kept for deductions when you sell your home. MaryJane put them in with her business type papers, but you can put them in this category if you wish.)

Appliances, (hanging file and plastic tab)

In here put the paperwork showing when you purchased the appliance, where, and how much it cost. You can put all of this information in one file folder, or separate it as shown below.

Q: For right now, put all appliance information in one file. If there's too much paperwork, then separate it out as shown. However, if you have very thick instruction books, do the following:

If you have thick instruction books, try putting them into medium or heavy-duty sheet protectors that you then put into a 3-ring binder. These sheet protectors can be bought at an office supply store and are a clear 3-ring pocket that opens at the top. You can slip the instruction book in it, as well as the warranty information. Staple your sales receipt to the book and you have everything in one convenient place. Remember to remove the book when you no longer have the item.

- Appliances, Large (hanging file)

- Dryer (file folder)

- Freezer (file folder)

- Refrigerator (file folder)

- Washer (file folder)

- Appliances, Small (hanging file)

- Microwave (file folder)
- Toaster Oven (file folder)

Accessories (hanging file and plastic tab)

- Bed Linens (file folder(s))
- Computers (file folder(s))
- Lamps (file folder(s))
- Radios (file folder(s))
- Stereo (file folder(s))
- TV's (file folder(s))

Furniture (hanging files and plastic tab)

- Bedroom (file folder)
- Dining Room (file folder)
- Kitchen (file folder)
- Living Room (file folder)

Information Papers

This is a wonderfully helpful category that MaryJane uses because it takes care of all those things that she doesn't have a clue what to do with, but wants to keep! We will use red hanging files, plastic tabs and file folders. These are papers that may be useful at some point in the future.

CAUTION

This is truly a temporary holding system where she puts information on things she might want to buy, places she wants to travel to, things she wants to see, and so forth. In here she goes strictly by the "A" to "Z" filing method. You can also arrange these files in categories, if you like. Again, these are your files, so put them in the easiest form for yourself. If you're not sure, try one way for a few weeks and see how it works. If you don't like it, change it

I also recommend that you label these file folders (not the hanging files) in pencil so that you can erase and reuse them when the information collected is no longer needed.

Q: Label hanging files from A to Z. Use pencil on all file folders that you put into these files.

Appliances (file folder that goes in the "A" hanging file)(Washer under "W," Dryer under "D," Refrigerator under "R," etc.)

MaryJane and John are collecting information on washers and dryers to replace their old ones. After they buy what they want, they will throw out the information they collected in this file and remove this folder from the "Information" area. The new washer and dryer information will be filed in the large appliance hanging file, or in a 3-ring notebook.

Decorating Ideas (file folder in the "D" hanging file), (Furnishings; Furniture; Things For The House, etc.)

With two young children, MaryJane dreams of new living room furniture and sees many pieces she would like to have. They can't afford to buy now, but want to buy within five years. MaryJane can put all her dreams and wishes into this file for future reference. Once she buys the particular piece she wants, she can remove the information from this file. She could possibly remove this folder from the file if she no longer needs to replace any furniture.

Entertainment (file folder that goes in the "E" hanging file)

You can put theater info here, amusement parks, mini golf locations, etc. Anything at all that interests you can be kept here.

Fencing (file folder that goes in the "F" hanging file)

Possible interest in getting a new fence. Any information that comes in the mail, or is picked up at home shows can go in this file.

General Activities; Dreams (file folder that goes in the "G" hanging file)

Jury Service (file folder in the "J" hanging file)

John keeps getting called to Jury Service and wants to keep a record of it.

Places To Go/Trips (file folder that goes in the "P" hanging file or the "T" hanging file)

Places of interest in your city or other cities. You could split this category into "Day Trips," "Weekend Trips," and Long Trips." Include maps and guides in this file. Again, this sub-division is entirely up to you.

Restaurants (file folder that goes in the "R" hanging file)

All the menus that you pick up from restaurants and fast-food outlets can go in this file. You can keep coupons here, but as you may forget them, keep them with your other coupons.

Roofing (file folder that goes in the "R" hanging file)

This couple needs to re-roof their home. They are investigating all the different types of roofing that they can use.

Again, once they re-roof they will transfer the specific roof information (purchase price, warranty, etc.) into their household records area and remove this temporary file.

Services (file folder or folders that go in the "S" hanging file)

Information that you collect, or is sent to you, on skilled workers, caterers, house cleaners, gardeners, government help and agencies.

Shopping Malls (file folder or folders that go in the "S" hanging file)

This file can be very important, especially when shopping for special occasions. If you go to other states for holidays, information on their shopping malls is also useful.

The next type of files to look at are your "Personal" papers.

Personal Papers

These files tell us all about MaryJane, her family and the people in her life. She has chosen blue hanging files, tabs and file folders for this grouping.

Education (hanging file and plastic tab) (School Records)

In this hanging file you can put everything pertaining to everyone's schooling, in their own file folders. You can keep graduation records, certificates of completion and continuing education certificates in here. These files can be sub-divided into baby years, preteen and teen years for the children, with school report cards, awards, etc.

Be sure to read the chapter on Children so that you know how to handle the artwork that the kids bring home. If you have lots of school memorabilia, consider storing it into plastic bins and putting it into a closet or in the garage with other memorabilia.

- April - Education (file folder)
- John - Education (file folder)
- June - Education (file folder)
- MaryJane - Education (file folder) ("Mine")

Q: Make a file folder for each person in your family and put any paperwork pertaining to each person in their own file folder.

Employment Records (hanging file and plastic tab) ("Work" or "Work Records")

You keep anything related to your work in this file: resumes, work history, evaluations, awards, promotions, etc.

- John (file folder)
- MaryJane (file folder)

Family/Relatives (hanging file and plastic tab) ("People We Have To Deal With," "People We Love," "Our Favorites")

Letters, cards, birth notices, invitations, likes and dislikes, sizes of clothing, etc., are some of the items you can put in these file folders. If you keep a great number of these, use two or more hanging files.

- Ann, Mother (file folder) (MaryJane's Mom) ("Mom")
- Bea, Mother (file folder) (John's Mom) ("Mother-In-Law")
- Bob, Brother (file folder) ("The Brat.")
- Sue, Sister (file folder)

Q: Keep all family information in one file folder.

Friends (hanging file and plastic tab) ("People We Like")

In this hanging file you can keep all those little birth announcements that you get from friends and feel guilty about throwing away. If the hanging file gets too full, consider putting this information and family information into two or more hanging files. Or you can use box bottom hanging files. You can keep all your friends in one hanging file, or use separate file folders for special friends.

Q: Keep all friend information in one file folder.

- Your name here - My Neighbor (file folder)

Notice that MaryJane made a file for you! The same information you keep on your family can be kept in these files for any friends you wish to keep tabs on.

- Sheila - My Organizer (file folder)

Aha! I've finally hit the big time! A file in the friend section!

Medical Records (hanging file and plastic tab)

Medical records can be kept in a separate file folder for every member of the family (including pets). If you feel that you need to divide this more because of many medical records, do so. Some clients divide theirs into annual exams, blood work, dentist, eye exams, mammograms, pelvic exams, prescriptions, shot records, surgeries and x-rays. If you have medical problems, dividing this group may be the best way of keeping your information together so that you can retrieve it quickly when you need it.

Q: Keep all medical information in a file folder for each person or pet.

As for your child's medical records – keep until the child is living on her own and then give it to her. Yes, you can. Just do it! (I kept a secret copy of their important illnesses, etc., in a safety deposit box and discarded them when I felt they were being responsible for their own health.)

- April - Medical (file folder)
- John - Medical (file folder) ("His")
- June - Medical (file folder)
- MaryJane - Medical (file folder)
- Pets - Medical (file folder)

Q: Keep all children's information in one file folder, pets in another.

Military Records (hanging file and plastic tab) (Once saw "Fighting" - ouch!)

MaryJane's husband served in the military and had all his assignments, promotions, awards and discharge papers in this file. If MaryJane had served in the military, a file folder for her would have been set up. (Unless you need these files active, it might be best to archive them – file them away in a good storage box with other memorabilia papers.)

- Military Records-John (file folder)

Religious Activities (or the name of house of worship) (hanging file and plastic tab)

- Choir Information (file folder)
  Rehearsal dates, performance dates, music, etc. can be in this file, but the dates need to be recorded on your calendar.

- Retreats/Seminars/Conferences Information (file folder) ("Getaways")

  Keep this information current unless you are doing an historical record

- Study Notes (file folder)

  If this folder gets large, put the study notes into a 3-ring notebook with dividers for each book or topic you are studying.

Volunteer Work (hanging file and plastic tab)

- John-Boy Scouts (file folder)

  Meeting dates and times, trips, telephone listings, names of the boy ` scouts and their parents names and numbers, etc.

- MaryJane - PTA (file folder)

  Meeting dates, special events, fundraisers, etc.

Hallelujah! We finally made it through the tough boring stuff! Take a breather and relax before tackling the rest.

Are you ready now for the Six-second marvel?

The Six-second marvel

If you set your files up the way that you think and speak, you'll be able to find the paper you're after within six seconds. My client, R.S., said, "No Way! That will never happen!" Well, when we finished setting up her files I tested her. I asked her to find the warranty papers on a new item she had just bought. She went to the file cabinet, pulled out the piece of paper, and handed it to me in four seconds! She couldn't believe it, so we did it again on some jokes she had collected. And she did it again in three seconds!

If your files truly reflect your lifestyle, anything is possible. But don't forget, files are like running water, ever-changing. What may be "OK" today may be outdated next year. Once your files are in place it'll be easier to streamline them. When you do your annual or semi-annual updating of your files, you can take a hard look at them to decide if you need to add, change, or delete files or categories.

The Daily Uglies

In order to tackle the daily uglies that you receive, I will discuss different ways of saving the information you need.

Though I've mentioned it already, I want to emphasize that you must have a calendar. If you do not have a calendar in terms of one you can write on, whether a date planner or a wall calendar, Get One! This is crucial to your success in this journey. Or, if you're "techie," you can use a computerized calendar.

If you like to see things right in front of you, you might want to consider putting some of your paperwork into files and sitting them between bookends. Or, files can be put into a stair-step file holder that is placed on top of a desk or counter so that you can easily see the files. If having the files right in front of you isn't important, you can put these same files into a desk drawer.

The purpose is to put paperwork into these files that need your immediate attention, or items that you don't want to forget. Examples of these items are: calls to make, errands to run, items to buy or return, etc. Many people put these items under magnets on the refrigerator or on a bulletin board. The bulletin board isn't bad if you don't have many things to follow-up on, but the refrigerator can become a nightmare of papers and I highly suggest that you don't entertain that idea.

(Bulletin boards are a convenient place to put things that you must remember for the next day. They are not designed for a year's worth of notices!)

You can call these files "Action" or "Project" files. Action items are more along the lines of returning phone calls or going to a theater performance, while project files are for specific projects you're working on, like remodeling your kitchen.

Some people also call these action or project files "Hot" files because to them they are hot and must be looked at. Another method to handle bills that need to be paid, follow-up calls, errands that must be run, etc., are "Tickler" files. Let's take a look at some tickler systems.

Tickler Files

One Tickler system is a set of file folders, labeled 1 through 31. The 1-31 dates are for specific deadlines within a given month. Another set of folders can be labeled January through December and these months are for nonspecific dates in a particular future month.

For example: If a performance at your church is scheduled for June 15, then you file the notice one week prior, in the file folder marked the 8th. This is to remind you that the performance is in a week. Remember to also record this in your planner for the actual date of the performance.

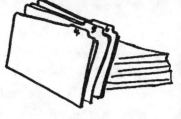

Then on the 8th you can move the notice ahead to the 14th, at which time you take it out and put it with other items you may be taking to your church on the 15th. Or tack it to your bulletin board, if you have one, or place it where URGENT items go.

Do this with anything you get that you want to go to. Let's say it's a performance in December, and this is November. You can file the information in the December folder and on the 1st of December you can take it out and file it under a date that is one week prior to the performance. I highly recommend that you mark it on your calendar.

If you find that filing a performance notice one week prior to the event just too much trouble, then file it the evening before the event. Filing it one week ahead just gives you a "heads-up" in case you forget to write it down in your planner.

These tickler files can be set up using clear plastic file folders instead of regular manila or colored files. The plastic files also come in colors and can be found at an office supply store. Since they are see-through, you have a visual reminder that something is lurking inside.

The clear plastic file folders for this system can also be placed in a stair-step file holder like we used for the Action/Project/Hot Files. These stair-step file holders are inexpensive, but be sure to buy the larger wire holder that is almost as tall as the files so that your file folders can't bend over the top.

Most of these wire vertical holders have 8 slots in them, so you can set up four days at a time in each slot. Put the 12 months in the last slot. The vertical holder then needs to be placed on an open surface or counter so that you can see it and be able to easily use it. You could put the file folders between bookends, but it is more difficult to use that way. If you don't like the idea of something sitting out, you can also put these files into hanging files within a desk drawer.

The tickler system is absolutely great for following up on phone calls and appointments. The down side is that you must look into the folders **Every Day.** Because I hate to look "into" something every day, I suggest using the plastic file folders and keeping only the ones that have something in them in the stair-step holder. You can turn the empty ones backwards at the end of the holder, or put them underneath the holder. It's easier to track five folders than 31.

Another tickler system that is useful if you have no room to keep file folders between bookends, in a stair step file holder, or on a bulletin board, is a door/wall-hanging calendar. This product is made out of heavy canvas and is called an "EZ Pocket." There are 31 pockets and two long horizontal pockets at the bottom for pens/pencils.

The calendar is not month dated. Each pocket has one day of the month on it (1, 2, 3, etc.). This item can be shipped directly to your home and you can get information on it by calling 1-800-681-8681. Ask for Carol or Frank and let them know I told you to call! They are located in Colorado and are very efficient at getting these items in the mail. They have other wall filing items also. Plastic pockets are also available elsewhere, but I cannot vouch for the durability and strength of the plastic.

Well, we've talked about filing and supplies and methods. It's now time to test you on what you've learned! Come on, it's an easy test!

Questions to Ask

When you sit down to process your mail, only open one piece of mail at a time and look at the contents. Ask each and every piece of paper the following questions. Yes, out loud!

- "Who are you from"?
- "What do you want"?
- "When do I have to take action"?
- "Where do I have to go"?
- "Why do I have to do this"?
- "If I file you, how will I find you"?

Let's Practice

Pretend the paper you just took out of the envelope is from the school's PTA (who are you from) and it's asking for your help (what do you want) in baking for the bake sale on Saturday (when do I have to take action).

If you're going to participate, put the bake sale date on your calendar or in your planner. Depending on how often you grocery shop, plan and note a few days ahead to buy whatever products you might need to bake and also note on your calendar when you're actually going to bake. Once in your planner you can throw the notice away.

The next piece of paper is from your mortgage company. It tells you how much you've already paid on your house and how much is left to pay.

This is a statement and can be filed because there is no action that you need to take; it's only information. However, the year-end statement will have to be kept with your tax papers to show how much interest you've paid.

If you don't have time to file this paper right now, take a pencil and in the upper right-hand corner mark where in your files you want this paper filed - in your Business papers, under "Mortgage." Pretend that you have a secretary that will be filing the paper for you.

This marking eliminates the need to constantly re-read everything you get. Place this paper in a special place for items to be filed (a filing tray, a desk drawer, a hanging file in the file cabinet or any other imaginative place you can think of). Now might also be a good time to train the kids how to file these papers for you! Back to the mail!

The next item of mail you have is from the eye doctor letting you know it's time to schedule an appointment.

Pull out your calendar, decide on a good day to call the eye doctor, and write it down. Now, what do you do with the reminder card?

You can throw it away, but if this frightens you, you can pull out a file folder (any color you like), and mark it "To Call." Put this between bookends, or preferably in the Hot File "stair-step" vertical file holder discussed above. The stair-step design allows you to put several file folders in the holder and still see all of them.

The next piece of paper you look at is an advertisement for a couch. Do you need a couch? If you do, but you can't buy it right now, put it in your "Information" category, maybe in a "Want to Buy" folder in the "W" hanging file, or even "Couch" in the "C" hanging file.

If you don't need a couch, throw it out! Yes, that's what the trash can is used for. If you do want to buy a couch as soon as possible, pull out a file folder and label it "To Buy." Put it with the other "hot" file folders. Remember: these file folders are temporary! They are meant to remind you that you need to do something with them. If you have a problem remembering that there is paper inside the files, buy some see-through colored plastic file folders just for this purpose. No more excuses! Back to the mail!

The next item you pick up is from your place of worship letting you know that there will be a special performance next month.

You really want to go. Pull out your calendar and mark it down. You have some options as to where to put the paper.

• You can staple it to your calendar.

• You can make another file folder called "Events," or "Special Performances," and put it with the other Hot File folders.

The next piece of mail is a credit card invoice from Visa. Get the sales slips from the envelope, holding area, or Hot File you are using to hold these sales slips.

Compare the sales slips with the invoice. If everything checks out then shred or discard the sales slips, except the ones you may need for income tax purposes. Put the invoice in any tickler system you're using seven to ten days prior to the due date. Mark this also on your calendar.

If you have a tremendous number of bills to pay, marking it on the calendar can get overwhelming, so you could just write "pay bills" on your calendar. If this is the case, having a file folder for "Bills" or putting them in a tickler system is probably best.

After your bills are paid, be sure to set aside the ones that you will need for your income taxes. I will discuss income taxes later in this chapter.

SIDE NOTE

All your credit card sales slips need to go in a holding place until the bill comes. You can use separate envelopes labeled with the account, e.g., VISA, for the various credit card slips.

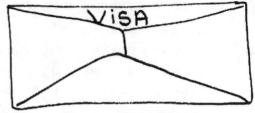

Do not put the slips all together in one envelope as it's a time waster when trying to check them against the invoice. Possibly the holding place can also be where you put your mail until you can open it, or you could keep them in an envelope in the credit card file. You could also put them in a Hot File, marked "Bills."

When next month's bill comes in, check it to be sure that your last payment is showing on it. If it is, and your slips match the invoice, then you can destroy the old bill. Unless you're retaining the credit card invoice due to a complaint, you do not need to keep the invoice once everything has been paid and you have no returns. Of course, if you have taxable items on the statement, then be sure to file it with your tax papers.

If you don't like the Hot File option, put the bill in the EZ Pocket (if you bought one). Be sure to put the bill in the pocket seven to ten days before the bill is due so there's time to write out the check and mail it. This also prevents late charges! By the way, because the EZ Pocket is not by month, you can use it for future months, if you wish. Just add it to the pocket.

If you don't like the Hot File, or the EZ Pocket, you can put the bill in your "tickler file." This is just another method to handle the important items that don't belong with your regular filing.

OK, where were we? Back to the mail!

There's a recall on your husband's truck and one of you has to take it to the garage. Put it on your calendar for when that's convenient and file the paperwork in the EZ Pocket, Hot File or tickler file.

You receive notice about construction in the area and that your street will be closed. Put it on your calendar and post the notice on your bulletin board or other area where urgent notices go. Be sure to inform everyone in the house. Inform others who may have to come to your home during that time.

You receive some catalogs. Not a surprise. Who doesn't? Now, I have a firm belief about catalogs, magazines, newspapers and the like. Once you've received three issues and the fourth one comes in, throw away/give away/donate the oldest one.

If you get catalogs monthly, you'll have one quarter of the year covered; if you get magazines once per quarter, you'll have a full year covered; and if you get periodicals yearly, you'll have three years covered. How many of these items do you receive?

Just think about it. Some of my clients have up to 20 catalogs delivered. They kept them "forever." They finally decide to buy an item, only to discover that it's no longer available! Take my urging and only keep three of each periodical, if you must keep any.

And newspapers can be thrown away daily because by the next day the news is old.

You receive a quarterly report on your IRA account. Check it against the last report you received to make sure the figures are accurate, and then file it.

Where? In the Business section. You can keep all these reports if you want, but they get bulky. Be sure to keep the initial one and every year-end report.

Your tenant sent their rent check. Log it into your business ledger, or computer program and make out a bank deposit slip. Put the check and deposit slip in the "Things To Do" folder in your Hot Files, the tickler file, on the bulletin board, or in tomorrow's EZ pocket date so that you remember to deposit the check.

Your new tenant finally signed the lease and mailed it to you. Put it in their file within your Rental category (Business section under Investments), and note on their tab, in pencil, the start and end dates of the lease.

You've just completed the mail for today. You want to file what just came in so that you don't have another backlog.

As the saying goes, "Rome wasn't built in a day," and you can't build your filing system in a day. It took you quite a while to have all that paper around you and it'll take quite a while to get it sorted and filed. Slow and sure is better than fast and unsure, or "haste makes waste." You will succeed. I promise you.

And here's something you may not realize. The only filing system that works for people with ADD/Dyslexia/Hoarding compulsions is our own! The magic of quick fixes and standardized filing just doesn't work for us. With my own system it's like having top secret documents and no one else can find them. Realistically they can, but it will take them longer than it takes me.

Unfortunately, your being a top secret agent will not work when you have to share filing space. Other styles of filing may be preferred. So if you're sharing filing space with your spouse or children, come to an agreement as to how your files are going to be categorized. All of you should be able to access the files without difficulty.

It's now time to start setting up your files on your own. Yes, you can do it!

"Do not be fainthearted or afraid; do not be terrified or give way to panic..." (Deuteronomy 20:3)

Decide on categories, and the colors you want to use, if any. You don't have to use colors, but it definitely makes things easier to find. Buy your hanging files, file folders and a file cabinet if you need one. Sort your papers into four piles and Go For It! Write out the subcategories you want, put your labels on your file folders and hanging files and put them in the filing cabinet. Wow!

But what about all the paperwork that's still scattered throughout the house? (Apparently you really did read this entire chapter and didn't pick up all your paper!)

Well, we go back to the beginning of setting up files. Remember that I said homes and businesses run on four types of files: business, household, information and personal? That's a clue. Gather all your paperwork into one location and separate it into these four types of categories.

I realize that some of you have a tremendous quantity of papers around, so maybe you had better get some big containers to hold it while you do this. Now I know that some of you think that if the papers stay spread out everywhere you don't have to worry about them or file them. But did you ever stop to realize that, in a sense, your life is spread out all over the place with no where to call "home"? That's sad. We all need a home and our papers need a home as well. Just gather the paper into the four piles. The Business pile is going to be the most important, so start filing those papers first.

A word of caution on filing. For the sake of your sanity, and those around you, set an alarm clock or timer for one-half hour when you're filing. If you find that you are perfectly okay after the half-hour, then set it for another half hour and then quit. Do not try to file beyond one hour. You may be able to, but you'll soon resent it because, like exercise, this is a task that you must do in order to "stay in shape."

If you cannot tolerate filing every day then do it, like exercise, a minimum of three times a week. Going to the gym once a month doesn't work, and filing once a month doesn't work. Please, Please, Please do not go on a marathon filing binge and try to do it all in one day. We with ADD tend to do the "all or nothing" routine, so heed my warning. You may never file again if you do it that way.

Now, let's test your new system. See yourself in this new scene:

You get your mail but don't have time to read it, or look at it, so you place it in your desk drawer (the holding area) that is strictly for your mail and nothing else.

If there are bills in your mail (and you know that they must be paid soon), you put a rubber band around the bills so you can spot them easily, or you put them in a secondary holding place (a smaller basket). This helps you get to them quickly when you need to pay them.

You decide that tomorrow, after you return from the kids' soccer game, that you will have at least one-half hour to go through the mail, so you mark it on your calendar.

Tomorrow is now today, you are home from the soccer game and you take your mail out of the drawer. Close by are your mail sorting supplies. You look through the mail, decide what needs to be discarded, acted on or filed, and you're through in 15 minutes! Wow! Just think how liberating that can be!

The final liberation is to have a place for papers you need for income taxes. Whether you do your own taxes or take them to an accountant, setting up tax files is Really Easy! Seriously!

Tax Files (part of your Business files)

- Get two sets of different colored filing folders, about ten each. One color will be for this year. The other color will be for next year and then you will alternate back to the first color and so on.

- Take out last year's tax records and look at the different schedules you used. You will set up a file folder for each of those schedules.

Let's look in on MaryJane again so that I can show you how to do this.

- MaryJane's first file folder is Income and all their earning statements are put in that file.

- In Janurary,or at least by the end of February, you should receive your wage earnings statements from your employer, or a 1099 from everyone you contracted with. If you're self employed you should have been keeping a written log or computer log of your clients/ customers to show how much money you earned.

The following file folders are what MaryJane uses each year. She alternates colors by the year. This year's files are in red. Next year's will be green. Then she will go back to red again. At the end of the current year, after you've done your taxes, file your taxes with all the supporting documents in a box bottom hanging file or in a large envelope.

That's why I said to buy two colors of file folders for taxes. By not dating them you can cycle them year after year. If a schedule is no longer needed, just remove that file folder. If a new one's needed, just add it.

- Business Expense (Her husband is able to write off some of his job expenses)
- Capital Gains/Losses (They buy and sell property fairly often)
- Donations (They give cash at church and checks to charities)
- Income (All W2's and 1099's)
- Interest Earned & Dividends Earned (Their savings account and stock income)
- Interest Paid (Monies paid out on their mortgage)
- Investments (Monies received from investments)
- Medical Expenses (Monies paid for all doctors, dentists and eye exams)
- Miscellaneous (Monies paid for car licenses, safety deposit boxes, etc.)
- Partnerships (Monies received from partnership investments)
- Telephone Expenses (A portion of the telephone can be written off for their rental business and for John's business)

These sets of files take up very little space in your file cabinet. They can even be put into a plastic carrying cases with a handle that accommodates hanging files.

As you set up your files according to your income tax schedules, you may have some of the above categories, or some very different ones. The objective is to keep all that paperwork in one place.

You may need only one hanging file to handle the file folders for the current year and one for the following year, (see explanation below). Since you don't access these records on a regular basis, they can be put in the bottom file drawer, in the top drawer if you're short and have a four-drawer file cabinet, or behind or in front of your business records.

The extra set of file folders will be for next year's files. The reason you want a duplicate set is so you don't wind up putting next year's income tax papers into this year's income tax papers. If you do your income taxes on the first of January, then you have no problem and don't need this extra set. If you wait until April to work on your taxes, or have your accountant work on your taxes, you're going to have paper coming in from January through April that will have nowhere to go.

It's easy with a duplicate set. If you have someone else do your taxes, they will be delighted that you have sorted the papers for them. Remember, you're paying them for every minute that they have to work on your tax return. If you can total up your income, donations, medical expenses, interest income, and so forth, that will save you even more money.

Don't let your taxes intimidate you. All you're doing is separating your tax papers into different file folders so that you or your accountant can do the income taxes. If you file a short form you will not have to worry about setting up these files. Once you own property, pay interest, earn interest or give money to charities, you'll probably want to file a long form and set up these files. Always check with your tax person about the best way to set up your files to make it easier on her/him.

Summary

- Remember that your home is a business.
- Have a holding place for mail and bills.
- Gather all papers into four piles: business, personal and information.
- Buy a file cabinet large enough to hold your records.

- Buy file folders, hanging files and tabs - in color if you wish.
- Talk to your papers about where they belong and if you need them.
- Talk to your mail about what they want you to do.
- Be realistic about discarding paperwork you no longer need.
- Keep four file folders available for the four types of paperwork you'll be collecting before you file.
- Think about a tickler system or Hot File system to track important items.
- Set up your tax files according to your old income tax records.

I Will:

- come to terms with the fact that papers also have a life cycle;
- have a holding area for my mail when I can't open it right away, and I will keep my bills in a separate holding area;
- mark every piece of paper that I want to file away so that I don't have to keep reading it again and again to decide what to do with it;
- I will put papers that need to be filed away into four file folders - one for business items, one for household items, one for information items and one for personal items;
- stay focused for at least one-half hour to decide on where to file items and another one-half hour on another day to file the papers;
- not become dis-trackted!

Enjoy your new home and know that you now can take care of it. Now say: I WILL ...BECAUSE I CAN!

Above and Beyond Clutter

Well, we've gone through most of the areas in your home and you have all your files and tax records set up. The "after" scene of chaos is this:

You walk in the front door and are thankful to be home. You know exactly where the groceries go and the kids keep their toys and school work in their rooms. Your husband's briefcase is on his desk and there are no peanut butter smears on your kitchen counter. Because the house is quiet, you sit down at your alcove in the kitchen, take your mail from your wicker basket and open your mail. You put a bill in your tickler system that needs to be paid next week, note on your calendar to call a friend on the weekend, and file a mortgage statement.

You start dinner and put a load of wash into the washing machine. The kids will put the wash into the dryer when they're through with their homework.

You feel rested and in control. Life IS good. Every day may not be wonderful, but you now know that everything has a home - and so do you!

"Even the sparrow has found a home, and the swallow a nest for herself..." (Psalm 84:3)

Even Martha Stewart knows this when she said, in Harper's Bazaar, "Life is too complicated not to be orderly."

CHAPTER 10

The Psychology of, and Reasons for, Clutter

Why We Clutter
An Interview With Melissa Thomasson, Ph.D.

According to Melissa Thomasson, Ph.D., a Licensed and Clinical Psychologist in Arcadia, California, who lives with ADD, there are two main categories to look at in relation to us and clutter:

1. **Psychological/Behavioral**: clutter challenges without Attention Deficit (ADD) issues or Learning Disabilities (LD).

2. **Neurological Basis**: clutter challenges with Attention Deficit (ADD) issues, Learning Disabilities (LD), or Memory Problems.

In this section she explores some of the common causes of chronic disorganization. This discussion is meant to give a general understanding of those common causes. It is not meant for self-diagnosis or diagnosis of others you know. Diagnosis of neurologically based conditions and personality structure should be done by a qualified professional such as a clinical Psychologist or Psychiatrist.

Psychological/Behavioral

Some people have poor organizing skills because they didn't learn how within their family structure. Their parents may have been chronically disorganized and lacked role models for using organization in daily living.

Included under the psychological/behavioral category are compulsive collectors who:

- prevent themselves from discarding possessions
- have too much to organize
- keep volumes of records, magazines, etc.

Causes of Being "A Collector" Include

- Very bright people with varied and passionate interests (have many books on many areas of interests, huge music collections, etc.);
- Having a Personality Type that can be made worse, or better, by their environment when growing up.
- Being taught to not throw anything away, to be thrifty, or that they may find a use for "it" someday. They may have come through the depression era (or raised by someone from this era), of collecting tin foil, rubber bands, string, etc.; and/or
- Depression. Grief or severe depression can bring memory and concentration problems causing people to lose things and become disorganized. The depression causes them to have little or no energy to do any organizing, but it is also depressing to be in an out of control environment.

Sometimes organizational problems show up in people who suffer from "co-dependency" or passivity. They don't set limits on other people's clutter. They can't tell children how to organize their rooms or possessions or how to set limits. Treatment: therapy, assertiveness training, marital counseling, or learning organizing skills for the family.

Personality Issues Affecting Organization

Type "A": Another common psychological profile affecting organization is the "Type A" personality. They can be involved in many projects with many responsibilities so there is little time to organize their lives.

Type A's may be bright with varied interests. Some read voraciously and have many books, large collections of records, etc. They also may have many hobbies and much "stuff." The spouse and family of the Type A clutterer may be upset with the disorganization. If these things were under control it could make life easier at home and they could relax if they were able to or chose to.

Neurological Causes

Right Hemisphere

People who are right-hemisphere oriented and holistic in their thinking may have difficulty with detail and follow through. The little details of life get put aside, like Accounting, which is a left hemisphere activity.

For many people who are right-hemisphere oriented and also have Attention Deficit Disorders, it is difficult to focus attention on details, making paperwork (which is a detailed left-hemisphere task) under stimulating

Right-hemisphere oriented people often like to be creative and act by inspiration. Some mundane organizing tasks are difficult to get inspired over because the tasks do not involve enough creativity.

Obsessive-Compulsive Personality

A personality type which includes an inability to get rid of worthless or worn out objects, and hoarding money or objects for future use. This personality type tends to focus on details and lists. They may be perfectionistic and can be stubborn and miserly.

Obsessive-Compulsive Disorder (a bio chemical imbalance problem referred to as OCD) is not the same as Obsessive-Compulsive Personality and is a separate disorder treated by medication and/or specific treatment programs.

Learning Disabilities Vs. Attention Deficit Disorders

Both Learning Disabilities (LD's) and Attention Deficit Disorder (ADD) are neurologically based, not psychological. Dyslexia (specific learning disability) occurs in 15% of the general population, according to The National Institute for Mental Health (NIMH). My estimate is that a good 10% of the general population has ADD. It is very common for those with ADD to also have some learning disability.

Learning disabilities are caused by differences of formation in the cerebral hemispheres. Attention Deficit Disorder involves differences in functioning of the brain stem and frontal lobes. The brain stem is the center of alertness, awakeness, focusing of attention, filtering out distractions, and switching focus from one task to another at will. Some facets of ADD that may lead to disorganization are:

- impatience with boring tasks
- difficulty prioritizing and making decisions
- impulsive placing of items
- lack of follow through ("it's too boring to hang up clothes, I'll do it later")

Memory problems are thought of by some as one specific Learning Disability while others write about memory problems as a part of ADD. For this discussion we can consider this an area of Learning Disability. Memory problems can range from mild, to moderate, to severe symptoms. Long or short-term memory problems can impact our everyday functioning:

- Where we put something;
- What we said we would do;
- Losing a telephone number;
- Recalling a sequence of doing something as in a computer program.

Some people with a Learning Disability in the area of memory are quite aware that they've had it all their lives. Others notice memory problems emerge only as life gets more complex. Normal aging also creates a slowing of memory processing, so as those with a Learning Disability in the area of memory have even more difficulty with memory. Less common causes of memory problems impacting organization can result from head trauma, stroke, or other neurological conditions.

Learning disabilities are present from birth, neurologically based, usually inherited or familial and presents some form of difficulty in left or right hemisphere functioning:

Left-hemisphere difficulties can include problems with reading, spelling, math, memorization of details (rote learning sequences), listening, verbal expression and written expression (processing language);

Right-hemisphere difficulties may include problems with musical tunes, reading facial expressions and tone of voice, social/behavioral cues (such as reading body language), sense of color and design, spatial awareness, and directionality;

Dyslexia is often thought of as a stereotype of letter reversals and severe problems with reading. Dyslexia can actually be left or right hemisphered in many different areas and can be from mild, to moderate, or severe. The term dyslexia is used interchangeably with Specific Learning Disabilities. Those with dyslexia have a "custom collection of symptoms" with some people having a few symptoms and others having a lot. The more symptoms we have the more they hamper our lives. The symptoms can be disabling and interfere with functioning in many areas of life.

People can "acquire" symptoms of learning disabilities or Attention Deficit Disorder through brain injuries from accidents, head trauma, or other neurological conditions. ADD can be with or without hyperactivity. In the current diagnostic manual (DSM-IV), all types of ADD are referred to as ADHD (Attention Deficit/Hyperactivity Disorder). This is confusing by many who think you must have hyperactivity to be called ADHD. I prefer to use the term ADD, with or without hyperactivity.

ADD with Hyperactivity (may or may not have organizing problems):

- Lack patience for the boring, organizing tasks
- Activity oriented (grasshopper approach - jumping from one incomplete task to another)
- Impulsive: acts on impulse
- Needs

ADD without Hyperactivity

- Problems focusing attention to start or finish tasks.
- Daydreams: may have frequent involuntary daydreaming or wandering thoughts. Also may have many ideas, thoughts but have difficulty putting thoughts into actions.

Both types have distractability issues. They will start one thing, do another, don't complete it or get off track. If there are memory problems, this can make the ADD problems much worse. An example would be going out to do the laundry and winding up in the back yard gardening. They get off track and can't remember the other track.

Both types have problems focusing on boring or anxiety provoking tasks. The difficulty doing boring tasks leads to disorganization and often detailed oriented tasks just don't get done (papers, etc.).

Distractability means that visual stimuli, auditory stimuli, or internal thoughts are difficult to filter out. This filtering problem makes it difficult to operate around noise, visual clutter or with their own internal distractors. Very often medication is the first line of treatment for ADD. Medication can help the person to focus and reduce their distractability. This in turn helps the brain in working better to learn organizational skills - starting and completing tasks without needing the excitement to do so. Even if they feel like throwing clothes on the floor, they actually put them away. This improvement in brain functioning helps their ability to focus on coping skills that strengthen through repeated use.

Breaking tasks down into smaller parts – how to make a list – how to prioritize, are easier to learn when they can focus. Without medication the strongest stimuli coming in is what they can easily focus on. If the task is under-stimulating it is difficult to focus on. If thinking about doing a task creates anxiety, then the anxiety creates another barrier to focusing on the task. If we have several equally powerful stimuli coming in it's hard to make a decision. Example: making a food choice in a restaurant. Several choices may seem equally appealing. This takes filtering, which is why it can be hard for those with ADD to prioritize.

For the Learning Disabled and Organization

Memory in organization (details, categorizing) is difficult but can be taught through coping skills and creating equipment such as an organizer book to strengthen functioning. Sequencing (recalling the order of procedures) can be another area of difficulty, but they can be taught through coping skills to improve functioning. Others have learned good coping skills as a child or developed them through the years.

Psychological/Behavioral Benefits of Organizing

Self-esteem depends in part from a sense of "mastery" and feedback from others. If we are disorganized, we may feel out of control, unsure of ourselves and our functioning, get negative feedback from others, and feel embarrassed or ashamed about our disorganized functioning. So, being disorganized often damages our self-esteem, and self-confidence.

Conversely, learning organizational skills and seeing our functioning improve in organization builds our self-esteem and self-confidence.

As we build our skills and see successes in this area, it helps us to become even more motivated in getting organized. By eliminating excesses our life gets back in control.

Often, relationships benefit from improving organizational skills:

- Spouses become happier with a more organized home;
- It reduces stress from lost things and clutter;
- Bosses are happy with our increased productivity;
- Friends are happier with our improved skills in returning a call;
- Being on time lets others know that you are considerate of their time;
- Following through;
- Sending a card shows thoughtfulness.

Treatment Strategies for Organizational Problems

Behavioral

When organizational problems are purely behavioral, the focus is on learning the basic skills of organizing. Then those skills are put to practice to help unlearn old behavior patterns of disorganization.

For "Type A" personality

Therapy stressing relaxation skills, time management, stress management and organizational skills.

For Chronic Depression

Medication and/or therapy.

For ADD

Medication is often very helpful along with learning time management, stress management and organizational skills.

Space analysis is used to help make decisions regarding how many items can be contained. An example would be an analysis of space for books. If one has 800 books but has space to store only 300, the resulting organizational problem becomes clear. Decisions must be made about what to keep, and what to give away. It is a rational/logical process. If there are expensive items that are not being used, they can be donated to libraries/museums so they can be seen and the person feels better about giving away their things. Or they could be sold for cash to go towards something worthwhile.

An example of an elimination procedure: If you decide to bring in five new books, also decide to eliminate five old ones. This helps to become motivated in getting organized because eliminating excess gets our life back in control. Getting organized is hopeful and empowering. It builds self-esteem and functioning.

There are few benefits to being disorganized or cluttered.

An Interview with Barbara A. Berg, LCSW

When asked during our interview what her schooled conception of clutter is, Barbara A. Berg, Licensed Clinical Social Worker, and a person living with ADHD, responded with the following clinical and personal insights:

- "No one makes clutter as fast as someone with Attention Deficit Disorder (ADD). Whether you're looking for one paper in particular or just trying to get out the door, anyone who has an issue with clutter can tell you they've got their reasons, and it's extremely difficult to alter the way things go.

- "While those living in Victorian times had 'planned clutter,' we who live in today's times have more stuff, and more clutter, in more places than the Victorian era inhabitants ever imagined. Today you can have clutter on your Email and your answering machine, along with your closets, under the bed and in file cabinets – not to mention in refrigerators, drawers, on desks, tables, shelves, fish tanks, anywhere imaginable. If there is space to store or hold anything, whether literally or figuratively, if you are inclined to have clutter in your life - it will be there.

- "One of the complexities of clutter is that different members of your family or work organization are bound to have different terms for it. Generally speaking, if the clutter is yours, you'll say 'It's my stuff.' If it is someone else's, you'll be inclined to call it 'junk.' Even if you don't need it and have no plans to ever use it, you'll probably see it as a 'treasure' of some sort, and another person will see it as 'trash.'

- "However, the kind of clutter I am speaking of here is the kind that gets in your way, that interferes with you achieving what you want. Consider these five psychological aspects of clutter. See which ones you can relate to:

A. Clutter often relates to how a person's mind really works. It can represent how much stress you have and how close to a brick wall you could be without even feeling it.

B. For instance, if you have cluttered files and you can't find anything or fit anything more in the drawer, you might also have a cluttered mind that doesn't get things done. You might have too many thoughts running around, and you don't realize how too much on your mind keeps you from effectively making decisions. Just like a cluttered file cabinet, a cluttered mind keeps you from knowing where things are when you need them. It's helpful to ask yourself, 'What's more important for me right now? Should I try to actually get something done, or is it worth my while to actually take time out and get organized.' Organization can help you clear your thoughts, which can lower stress.

C. It's easy, especially for someone with ADD or ADHD, to think that clutter should just take care of itself. Besides, it's a pain to go through a pile of chaos piece by piece. This is especially true if you don't have a place for everything to go. Some folks get in the habit of waiting a long time until the dates all expire, and then just throw it all away. If you have a pile, and you're afraid to attack the whole thing, just deal with five things at a time. You could take the approach, you do not care enough to create a space for something, so just throw it out. You probably won't miss it.

D. You may notice that you have clutter in some parts of your life and not in others. There's a good chance that the places where you have clutter represent aspects of your life you'd rather avoid. Unopened mail can be downright scary! So, too, can an overstuffed closet. Consider buddying up with a friend who'll accompany you while you venture into the woods and find out what's been hiding there. It's much more frightening to fantasize about what you're not facing that to confront it head on. You might be surprised to find something lovely you've forgotten or thought you'd lost.

E. Clutter can have a way of making you late for everything. If you have an issue with being on time, a cluttered closet can keep you from wanting to go anywhere. Being late always puts you at a disadvantage. You start each encounter with an apology or an excuse, and never quite catch up after that. Make cleaning your closet an exercise in selecting items for the resale shop, or supporting your favorite charity, or clothing the homeless. If you approach thinning out your wardrobe as a feel-good situation instead of a punishment where you are forced to give up things you might prefer to keep, space will open up in a hurry, and as the closet becomes organized (go ahead and treat yourself to new hangers!) you can look forward to a better social life. You'll have coordinating outfits at the ready, and will be able to show up unruffled and on time.

"Clutter can often be a message to others that what you are doing and when you get around to it is not important. It can imply a cavalier approach to life. For me, as an author, speaker, social worker, wanna-be standup comedienne (and more to the point, a person who is often plagued by ADHD), I have recently come to see that clutter which is out of my control is not a sign of success (I am sooo busy, so much in demand). The cluttery corners in my life (and believe me, I have them) are barriers that keep me from taking advantage of the opportunities life has to offer me. At 46, I realize that it is high time that I get rid of any-thing that is getting in my way, especially obstacles of my own making. I have set aside one evening a week, when my daughter has homework and I have a household aide, to dedicate to organizing my papers, my office, my life. After all, my clients, friends, daughter and readers are worth it and so am I. And so are you!"

Views of
the Author

Sheila G. McCurdy, CLUTTER STOP®
Personal Organizing Services for Homes and Offices

When I give seminars, a recurrent question that arises is, "Are there certain people who are more prone to clutter or have a personality that is more prone to clutter?" While I am not a therapist, I have talked to many counselors about why people create chaos wherever they go.

The two therapists I interviewed for this book gave fairly similar reasons for the how and why of clutter. As an organizer, I have talked to many people whose lives have been torn apart by disorganization. So, to add to what the therapists have discussed, I would like to share what I have learned from my clients, along with my personal observations of clutter, historically and futuristically.

Where it Starts

Removal of possessions. My clients are crowded with clutter for a variety of reasons. The biggest reason stems from their childhood. A concerned parent, or caretaker, decided that a toy their child was playing with was "too young" for them. Somehow, magically, the parent knew that the child was emotionally ready to move on and give up this treasured toy. This scene is repeated by too many parents to count. They pack up their children's belongings and throw them away without a second thought, usually over the loud protests of their child. Is it any wonder that as an adult this same child says "No, you're not going to throw my stuff out!"

Emotional pain. Other clients build walls of paper, literally. They stack and stack and stack until they have nice rows which, in some instances, become mazes. Their reasons? When they get through crying, they tell me the walls are a shield from further emotional pain. Since the walls represent protection, the more walls, the better the protection.

Physical pain. Some clients build walls and mazes as a barrier protection from physical and/or sexual abuse suffered as a child. It seems that both severe emotional and physical/sexual abuse causes people to build walls. And what is amazing is that many of these people haven't a clue as to why they collect papers/items and build walls with them.

Loss of control and trust. What I have observed over the years is that the clutter is an OPEN OBVIOUS DISPLAY of some deep emotional hurt. If therapy isn't sought to address these issues, it is very difficult to become organized. And with therapy, the organizing process is slow because the client needs to carefully work through the fear that comes with the supposed loss of control. There is also the issue of trust. If the client can't trust the organizer to help them, then there is a standoff and work cannot proceed. This is neither the client's fault, nor the organizer's. We all have different personalities and some just don't mesh. It just means that the client either needs another organizer, or additional therapy.

Training issues. Besides the walls that clients erect are the messes that "normal" people put up with. Normal meaning not hindered by Learning Disabilities, etc., that plague the rest of us. When these clutter problems occur, it is generally because no training took place when these adults were children. This training is so crucial and yet it is totally overlooked and not even given a passing thought by parents or caretakers. And the schools certainly don't teach "Organizing 101!" In my personal humble opinion, I feel that there are two things that children in school need to learn, or at least hear about, and those are parenting issues and organizing issues.

What Will Help

Working with children has proven to me that the schools are not educating our kids in the areas of organizing their schedules, their notebooks or their homework. So it is left to harried parents who don't understand the need themselves, or to organizers called in by those same harried parents. And all it takes are some simple instructions to the kids, who really catch on much quicker than we adults. Most of them know the areas that are troubling them, they just want help in fixing it.

By the time we reach adulthood we are "set" in our ways, having learned the best and the worst of whatever we experienced as children. Only through a slow process of therapy and/or behavior modification are we able to shift our ways of doing and looking at things. But **The Floor Is Not An Option!** helps in that process. This book is a basic primer for anyone with clutter and focuses in on those having additional difficulty through Attention Deficit Disorders, dyslexia, hoarding issues, Learning Disabilities and physical disabilities. And, sorry, but there are no cute acronyms for you to remember. I want to help you understand how to deal with your clutter without the added burden of remembering what "steps" you are supposed to follow or what sequence comes before what.

However, if you really like acronyms, then try this one: HELP! Translated, this stands for – Hearing Enhances Learning Possibilities!

Appendix One

Resources for:

Home Supply Stores (for storage containers & household items)

Container Store	(800) 733-3532
Hold Everything	(800) 421-2264
Lechters Housewares	(800) 605-4824
Lillian Vernon (catalog)	(800) 285-5555
Linens & Things	(800) 568-8765
Variety Stores: Target, K-Mart, Wal-Mart	check local telephone book
Home Repair: Home Depot, Orchard (OSH)	check local telephone book
Household Needs: Bed, Bath & Beyond	check local telephone book

or call the corporate office at 908-688-0888 for a store near you.

Office Supply Stores (for files & Pendaflexes)

Office Depot	(888) 463-3768
Office Max	(800) 788-8080
Staples	(800) 333-3330

Planning Calendars (for tracking your life)

At-A-Glance	(888) 302-4155
Day Runner	(800) 232-9786
Day-Timer	(800) 225-5005
EZ Pocket	(800) 681-8681
Franklin	(800) 654-1776

Professional Help – Finding an Organizer in Your Area

NAPO Hotline (National Association of Professional Organizers) (512) 206-0151

Sheila McCurdy, CLUTTER STOP® (909) 985-4948

Websites/Email – On-Line Information on ADD and Learning Disabilities

www.chadd.org (Children and Adults with ADD)

www.ldonline.org (Learning disabilities information and newsletter)

www.oneaddplace.com (Resource for ADD information, organizers, products)

www.add.org (Same as above – additional resource)

BrandiV'ns.net (ask for newsletter and information on chat groups for those with ADD/ADHD)

Appendix Two

Reading resources for ADD, Dyslexia and Learning Disabilities

Answers to Distraction. Hallowell, Ed, and Ratey, John. Pantheon Books, 1994.

Are You Listening? Fowler, Rick and Jerilyn. Thomas Nelson Inc., 1995.

Brilliant Idiot. An Autobiography of a Dyslexic. Schmitt, Aabraham, Dr. Good Books, 1994.

Driven to Distraction. Hallowell, Ed, and Ratey, John. Simon & Shuster, 1994.

Smart but Feeling Dumb. Levinson, Harold, M.D. Warner Books, Inc., 1994.

The Twelve Steps: A Guide For Adults With Attention Deficit Disorder. Friends in Recovery. RPI Publishing, Inc., 1996.

You and Your ADD Child. Warren, Paul, and Capehart, Jody. Thomas Nelson, 1995.

You Mean I'm Not Lazy, Stupid or Crazy? Kelly, Kate, and Ramundo, Peggy. Scribner, 1993.

What does everybody else know that I don't? Novotni, Michele, Ph.D. (Social Skills help for Adults with AD/HD) ADD Warehouse, 1-800-233-9273.

Women with Attention Deficit Disorder. Solden, Sari. Underwood Books, 1995.

Or, call ADD REsources for a free catalogue on books for adults and teens with ADD. (800) 409-4908

Appendix Three

How to Find a Coach (someone who helps you with your daily goals)

ADDCA – ADD Coach Academy

David Giwerc

(518) 482-3458

www.addca.com

American Coaching Association

Susan Sussman, M.Ed.

293 Birch Drive

Lafayette Hill PA 19444

(610) 825-8572

(610) 825-4505 fax

Susan.Sussman'compuserve.com

web: http://www.americoach.com

Susan Sussman belongs to the National Association of Professional Organizers (NAPO) and offers coaching, as well as training, for ADD coaching.

Catalytic Coaching

Sandy Maynard

(202) 884-0063

www.sandymaynard.com

Coach University

1971 West Lumsden Road, Suite 331

Brandon FL 33511

(800) 48COACH

Web: http://www.coachu.com

They train coaches and have a referral program.

Life Coach

124 Waterman Street

Providence RI 01906

(800) 253-4965; (508) 252-4965

Web: http://www.iquest.net/greatconnect.com/lifecoach

Techniques developed by Dr. Hallowell who wrote Driven to Distraction and Answers to Distraction.

OFI – Tho Optimal Functioning Institute

Founder: Madelyn Griffith Haynie

ADD Coaching Training

(865) 524-9549

mgh@addcoach.com

www.addcoach.com (start here)

Shadow Coaching

Thom Hartmann

(802) 229-2288

www.shadowcoaching.com

All of these refer coaches. You will need to speak to all three to get a clear idea of what a coach can do for you, how much time you will need to spend with them, and how much it will cost. You can also find independent coaches in your local telephone book. Be sure to ask for credentials and references on anyone you decide to work with. The results are up to you. They coach ...you play the game ...hopefully to win!

Glossary

Acronyms: Words formed from the first letters of a name or saying.

ADD (Attention Deficit Disorder): A neurological problem causing issues with, among others, focusing and follow-through.

ADHD (Attention Deficit Hyperactivity Disorder): A neurological problem causing issues with, among others, patience and doing things impulsively.

Audio Cassettes: Tape recordings that are listened to.

Baby Grand Piano: A very large piano whose lid opens up and is used for concerts. In a home it is usually placed in the middle of a room because of its size.

Behavior Modification: To make behavioral habits less extreme, severe or strong.

Behavioral: Learned behavior.

Bunkbeds: Two beds that either sit atop one another or where one is at an angle beneath the other.

Camouflaged: Concealing items by making them appear to be a part of the background.

Categorize: To classify into defined divisions.

CDs: Compact computer disks played on disk players and computers.

Changing Table: A table designed to hold a baby while changing diapers.

Chiffarobe: A combination chiffonier and wardrobe that results in a piece of furniture that has drawers and a separate cabinet for hanging clothes.

Chiffonier: A narrow, high chest of drawers or bureau, often with a mirror attached.

Clothes Rack: A portable stand, possibly with wheels, on which to hang clothes.

Clutter: To litter or pile in a disordered or confused state.

Co-Dependent: Two individuals who are totally dependent on the other.

Collectibles: A group of objects or works to be seen, studied, or kept together.

Collector/Hoarder: Keeping many things as a result of behavioral or psychological reasons.

Colorizing: Using colors to identify people or things.

Comforters: A blanket that is filled with material that gives it a fluffy appearance and can be used as a bedspread doesn't fall to the floor.

Communal Living Areas: All the areas of a home except the bedrooms.

Compulsive Hoarders (Packrat): To gather or accumulate by saving or hiding.

Condiments: Typically things that go on sandwiches – mustard, mayonnaise, ketchup, etc.

Cubbies: Plastic or wooden square boxes that can be aligned one atop another.

De-Cluttering: To put in order.

Depression: Caused typically by emotional issues which result in lack of concentration and organizing problems.

Dimmer Switch: A dial on a light switch that allows lights to be dimmed.

Disorganization: Lacking order or arrangement.

Dividers, Index Tab: A heavy 3-holed sheet of paper that is used in notebooks to separate sections of work. The index tab is used to label the divider for ease of finding the sections.

Dyslexia: A neurological problem causing issues with, among others, reading, spelling, directions and understanding what is read or heard.

Etagere: A piece of furniture with open shelves for ornaments. Some have drawers.

File Folder/Interior File Folder: An item about 8 1/2 inches wide and 17 inches long which is folded in half and has a cut out section at the top that creates a place to write on. It is made out of heavy paper that is used to hold papers. Usually used within a Pendaflex. An interior file folder does not show outside of the Pendaflex.

Hoarding Compulsions: Needing to keep items without knowing why.

Home: The place where an object can always be found.

Hot Files: Files used for items that need immediate attention.

Hummel Figurines: Small childlike sculptured statuettes.

Lladro Figurines: Dainty sculptured statuettes.

Incorporated: United into one body.

Instincts: Natural impulses.

Inventory List: A list that is used to keep track of items that will need to be replenished.

Leaders: The clear part of the tape on an audio cassette.

Learning Disability: Present from birth, neurologically based, usually inherited and can cause problems with reading, spelling, math, memorization of details, listening, verbal and written expression, problems with musical tunes, reading facial expressions and tone of voice, social/behavioral cues, sense of color and design, spatial awareness, and directionality.

Left Hemisphere: The left side of the brain, where details are stored.

Memory Problems: The inability to remember where something is put, what was said, or recalling details of one's life.

Miracle: An unexplained wonderful event.

Mission: A self-imposed duty or aim.

Neurological: Based in either or both of the left and right hemispheres of the brain.

Oasis: A small place preserved from surrounding unpleasantness.

Obsessive-Compulsive Disorder: Preoccupation with a fixed idea or unwanted feeling or emotion, often accompanied by symptoms of anxiety.

Obsessive-Compulsive Personality: Focusing on details and lists.

Organization: Having order and arrangement.

Paddy Wagon: A police van used in the mid 1900's.

Paper Shredder: An electric tool that sits atop a wastebasket and is used to shred papers.

Passivity: Accepting demands placed on one's self without objection.

Pedestal Table: Usually a round table whose legs are beneath the middle of the table rather than on the edges.

Pegboards: Corrugated fiberboard pieces that have holes in them to put hangers for tools or kitchen utensils.

Pendaflex: A heavy file folder with metal rods at the top and hangs in a file cabinet.

Permanent Marker: Markers that are used on clothing so that markings don't wash off.

Personality Types: Different personalities that create their own organizing issues.

Phonograph Records: A large breakable disk with recorded music that is played on a phonograph machine. Has been replaced by audio tape cassettes and compact disks (CDs).

Pillow Sham: A fancy cover for pillows that usually match a bedspread or comforter.

Possessions: Things that are owned.

Right Hemisphere: The right side of the brain, where creativity is stored.

Rubble Strewn: A total mess.

Sanctuary: A sacred place.

Self-Confidence: Feelings of self-assurance.

Self-Esteem: Respect for one's self.

Serenity: Unclouded and bright.

Sheet Protectors: A plastic 3-hole clear envelope that can open at the top or side. Usually used to protect important paperwork.

Stair-Step Vertical File Holder: A file holder that has separate levels so that you can easily see the file sitting behind the one in front.

Stress: A mentally or emotionally disruptive or disquieting influence.

Studio Piano: A smaller piano that can be placed against a wall.

Stuff: Household or personal items or worthless objects.

Tickler File: A series of files numbered for each day of the month and for each month of the year to act as a follow-up or follow-through reminder system.

Turntables: Plastic round plate-sized disks that turn like a lazy susan.

Type A Personality: The individuals take on many projects and responsibilities so they have little time to organize.

Utensil Holders: Small wall racks with hooks or small plastic narrow bins that fit in drawers.

VCR: Video cassette recording player.

Video Cassettes: Tapes that are played on VCRs and viewed on a television screen.

White Noise: Sound used to drown out other unpleasant noises.

Sheila McCurdy started her organizing business in March 1993 after leaving the corporate arena in 1991 as a Human Resources Director. While in various management positions, Sheila organized many offices and departments, streamlining paperflow and improving productivity.

Today Sheila spends most of her time organizing for those with Attention Deficit Disorder (ADD), dyslexia, learning disabilities and hoarding issues. Having ADD, she is acutely aware of the need for organizing solutions that will help those with ADD lessen their stress and anxiety, both at home and in the office. If one solution doesn't work, Sheila can quickly find another. She also helps mothers teach organizing methods to their children.

Sheila speaks before many ADD groups, for adults as well as for parents of ADD children. in addition to many other non-ADD speaking engagements. She is available for seminars, classes and workshops for home and office organizing and has given many seminars throughout southern California and to national and local conferences for the National Association of Professional Organizers.

CLUTTER STOP®
P.O. Box 2014
Upland, CA 91785-2014

909-985-4948
sheila@clutterstop.com
www.clutterstop.com